WHY DOES MY BOSS HATE MY WRITING?

WHY DOES MY BOSS HATE MY WRITING?

20 Questions that Can Help You Improve Your Business Writing 100 Percent!

BECKY BURCKMYER

Adams Media Corporation
Holbrook, Massachusetts

3 1257 01305 8861

Published by
Adams Media Corporation
260 Center Street, Holbrook, MA 02343

ISBN: 1-58062-057-4

Printed in Canada.
J I H G F E D C B A

Library of Congress Cataloging-in-Publication Data

Burckmyer, Becky
Why does my boss hate my writing? : twenty questions smart
business writers ask before they print / by Becky Burckmyer.
p.   cm.
Includes bibliographical references and index.
ISBN 1-58062-057-4
1. Business writing. 2. Commercial correspondence. I. Title.
HF5718.3.B87   1999
808'.06665—dc21   98-26691
CIP

This book is available at quantity discounts for bulk purchases.
For information, call 1-800-872-5627
(in Massachusetts, 781-767-8100).

Visit our home page at http://www.adamsmedia.com

Table of Contents

Introduction

This book is for you if you're having trouble with your writing at work. It's also for you if you're the boss and know something's wrong with the piece of writing that arrived on your desk this morning but can't put your finger on the problem.

Those of you having trouble writing: I empathize. For most of us, writing is an extension of ourselves. It's personal, and criticism is painful. I know: as an editor, I'm held to strict, if not punitive, writing standards. A casually e-mailed "Let's do lunch" is liable to elicit the reply, "Shouldn't that be 'Let us have lunch'?" It smarts amazingly. This book will teach you how to improve your writing and avoid the worst of the criticism.

Bosses: I empathize. I read lots of writing that needs help. And often it's very hard to zero in on exactly what's wrong. This book will enable you to criticize objectively and helpfully—unlike the boss in the following True Horror Story.

A senior vice president in a large financial institution once asked me to present a series of writing seminars targeted to upper management, herself included. Because I knew she was a good writer, I asked why she wanted help. Her boss had become increasingly critical of her writing, she replied. His latest way of expressing his feelings was seriously over the top. She had put a memo on his desk for his review and returned from lunch to find the memo on her desk—in a hundred tiny pieces. He had shredded it. Agreeing this didn't qualify as constructive criticism, we said bad things about him for a while, then planned the course. Later I got to thinking.

If you're like many people, though your writing may not literally get torn to pieces, your boss or manager may be returning it for rewrite with similarly unhelpful or inadequate explanations. You may get such vague comments as "It seems wordy," or "The language just isn't right," or if someone's been reading *The One-Minute Manager*, "I think you've got a good start here," meaning "It's lousy."

I've written this book to try to help. The chapters that follow lay bare what experience has convinced me are the Top 20 mistakes to avoid in business writing.

Most people in the business world are under too much time pressure to pause, review the rules of good writing, then practice them faithfully as they churn out letters, memos, e-mail, and reports. It's just not realistic. Yet for most people nowadays, writing well is not automatic. They start at the wrong end of the story; their mechanics—grammar, punctuation, treatment of capital letters and numbers—are not well founded; and they commit errors of style and coherence. Unfortunately, such writing can distract and alienate readers. Particularly discriminating readers can take a dislike to what you say because of the way you say it, and move on to assail, slash, and burn the *content* of your work. This is particularly true if you have a manager who has an intense personal relationship with grammar and style. A number of them do, and that shouldn't surprise us: good writing helps you get to *be* a manager.

If you're uncomfortable in the business writing you do, this book offers a solution. Go ahead and write: get it all down on your word processor as fast as you can. Then run through this "20-Step Program," which effectively makes you a copyeditor for your own work.

Why Does My Boss Hate My Writing? will give you a fact-centered, measurable way to go back and make your piece of writing convincing, communicative, and free of faults. Everyone needs to do this. Yes, even if you *are* under a lot of pressure. We all are: but this will take very little time, and it's quality time, well worth it.

In the questions that follow, I've targeted what I consider the 20 most jarring problems of style, tone, grammar and punctuation, and appearance with which I have become familiar in my work as a business writer, editor, and teacher. I didn't say the most important. Some of the errors are major, others are very small. But all of them will make your boss and anyone else who reads your writing hate it. These 20 chapters highlight the mistakes that readers of all kinds—from company executives to customers—tell me again and again really bother them. There's a lot to be said for writing *defensively,* that is, not bothering people. You don't want to make your reader aware of the act of reading because of something that grates or distracts. Accordingly, the act of writing should be as seamless as possible.

I don't pretend this book tells you everything. It's not designed for beginners, although someone with poor writing skills would benefit from reading it. If you're in trouble with the basics (what is a sentence, what is a subject, etc.), you need a comprehensive style manual and the time to research it: I've listed my favorites for you in

Appendix F. But I guarantee that if you work through the 20 questions, your writing will dramatically improve.

I realize nobody likes revising. The word has the smack of sincere and major tedium. But I think as you work with these questions, you won't feel as if you're revising, which is abstract and hard. You'll simply be running through 20 steps, one after another, which is concrete and easy.

I hope you're not getting harassment at the memo-shredding level. But if your manager, client, or colleague isn't satisfied with your writing, bang out your first drafts, then whip through this book before you print your final copy. You'll quickly learn which questions tend to trip you up and which ones you effortlessly get right. From first draft to finished product should become a quick and easy progression. You'll discover the faultfinders simmer down as their confidence in you rises. And you'll gain confidence in your writing ability as well.

If you're a manager, take a look at *Why Does My Boss Hate My Writing?* I suspect you'll find these chapters pick up on the issues that concern you in the writing your people do. You'll be able to recognize errors easily and deliver criticism objectively. And once you've identified and labeled specific problems that recur, you're well on your way to eradicating them.

Finally, a word to everyone: just be thankful if English is your native language, or if you learned it before your cortical layer (or wherever we store language) hardened. Experts tell us English is incredibly difficult to learn, and I believe it. A Japanese student in one of my business writing seminars asked, "Is the plural of 'horsepower' 'horsepowers' or 'horsepower'?" See? It could be a whole lot worse.

If your boss isn't happy with your writing, or if you're unhappy with someone else's writing, read the book through first so you understand each of the questions. Then begin using it. Simply scan the bold type, which will focus you on the issues before you print/critique. Good luck! I hope you enjoy *Why Does My Boss Hate My Writing?* and find it helpful.

CHAPTER ONE

Have I Written for My Audience?

In their classic for college students, *The Elements of Style*, William Strunk and his prize pupil E. B. White give the best writing advice you can get for $5.95—it's more than worth it at any price. Probably the single most important rule they offer is "Write for your reader." The advice sounds simple—like E. B. White's writing, deceptively so. Writing for your reader has many facets, and if you fail to bear them in mind, not only your boss but *all* who read your writing will hate it. Don't let this happen to you. To write for your reader means the following:

■ **Look through the reader's eyes.** First, it means seeing from the reader's point of view. Not a natural move, actually. When we write, we're intuitively focused on our own feelings, responses, and viewpoints. We're eager to bring people around to seeing things as we do. But believe me, when you are writing in hopes of pleasing, convincing, or otherwise capturing readers, it is no time to be selfish. Resist the temptation, realizing that for the reader, *the reader's* point of view is paramount. True to human nature, most readers are at least subconsciously asking themselves some version of the question, "What does this have to do with me?" or "Why is this writer writing this to me?" or the still more basic cry from the interior, "What's *in it* for me?" So, to paraphrase John F. Kennedy, ask not what your reader can do for you, but what you can do for your reader.

How can you tell whether you are looking at your message from the reader's point of view? This is not really difficult. Just ask yourself what effect this news will have on the person. If it's beneficial—we're offering you a better price, we're sending you a check, we're improving service—bring it out. Run it to the left-hand margin of your first line. Make it sharp, brilliant if you can. That's the hook with which you snag the reader.

> Dear John:
> Good news! Bergstrom has awarded you the contract to develop the 40 acres adjoining Route 2 as a high-end housing complex. I enclose, for your signature . . .

> Dear Mr. Jones:
> We're delighted to report your X-rays show no sign of any tumorous growth. At this point, we can conservatively say you are in remission and can reasonably anticipate no recurrence of . . .

> Dear Ms. Carey:
> Congratulations! You scored a nearly perfect 99 on your exam. This outstanding score qualifies you for advanced placement in Dr. Johnson's seminar next semester as well as . . .

> Dear Ms. Tuttle:
> Our records show you are correct: CountyBank inadvertently debited your checking account for a check drawn on your mother-in-law's account. Please accept our apologies and the enclosed receipt, which credits your account . . .

If, on the other hand, your news will have a negative impact on the reader, your task is to be sensitive. That means you probably shouldn't lead off with it—confronting the reader with your bad news. Suppose, for example, you need to tell Mrs. J that she didn't get the job she wanted with your company. Here's how *not* to do it:

> Dear Mrs. J:
> We're sorry, but the programming job went to another applicant. We rejected your application for these reasons.

Pushing the bad news to the fore is hurtful and makes for a painful read. You don't want to do this to your reader—not only because it isn't nice, but because it makes better business sense not to go around creating pain, which can translate into antagonism. Who knows? You might want to hire Mrs. J in another capacity. Or maybe your first applicant says no, and Mrs. J begins to look better. Very few of us are powerful and autonomous enough to go around alienating people without considering the consequences. Here's a better way to do it:

> Dear Mrs. J:
> Thank you for submitting your application for the programming job. As it turned out, we had a tremendous number of applicants for the position,

many of them with advanced courses and years of experience behind them. We must therefore . . .

Yes, she sees it coming. But at least she's being let down gently and politely. That's your responsibility as a writer.

There's another good reason not to push bad news up front. It can cause your reader to ignore the rest of your message, even though it may contain an explanation, helpful advice, or possibly good news. Here's an illustration that I wouldn't believe if it hadn't happened under my own roof. As a high-school senior, our son Charlie received a letter from a college to which he'd applied—we'll call it ST University—that began like this:

> Dear Charles:
> We are sorry to tell you that . . .

"Didn't get into STU, Mom," said Charlie, who had luckily been accepted where he'd hoped to go. He tossed the letter onto the pile of paper under which we think he has a desk. It surfaced six months later while I was looking for something else, and idly I scanned it. Of course you can guess what's coming. Somewhere around the fifth paragraph, I read:

> If you are interested in entering STU in January, we
> would be pleased to have you. However, we need
> to know your decision immediately . . .

Moral: always finish reading a letter. That's not my point here, however. My point is that STU had in fact *accepted* Charlie, and we didn't even know it. It didn't matter that much to us—but to someone else, it might have made a tremendous difference.

Sadly, this letter, a form doubtless sent to many applicants, could serve as a monument to writer-centered organization. Rather than considering what the reader needs to know or wants to hear, the writer has heedlessly spilled out the facts, probably in the order in which they came to mind. Result: not only writing that hurts, but a total failure to communicate.

Watch your level. Second, writing for your reader means hitting the reader's level. Your writing must be targeted to audience level in two ways. It must tap readers' level of *education*. Are you writing to high school graduates? College graduates? Grocers? Doctors? Teachers? It makes a difference. If you know to whom you are writing—at least predominantly—be sure your syntax, vocabulary, and length and complexity of sentences are geared to match.

Your writing must also tap readers' level of *knowledge*. In your occupation, avocation, and/or profession, you have probably already attained what I call the Dangerous Level of Knowledge, or DLK—you have become an insider. Your readers, on the outside, may or may not be as knowledgeable as you are. I use the word "dangerous" because when people become experts, they're no longer easily able to distinguish what others don't know. As a result, they risk failing to get their message across to readers. That's dangerous for everybody.

At the simplest levels, if you forget about the DLK, you may write elliptically. You may leave out something—because it's obvious to you—that is crucial to making your message clear to an outsider:

> Dear John:
> I look forward to meeting you on Friday morning, as you suggested, although of course Maureen won't be available to join us at that time.

Of course. Hello? Our writer neglected to consider that John didn't know, when he suggested a Friday meeting, that Maureen meets with senior staff every Friday morning. Familiarity breeds contretemps unless you're on guard against the DLK.

It gets more complex than that, of course. Consider this, which I stole, almost verbatim, from a local bank's direct-mail copy:

> And here's the best news of all. When you're a CountyBank customer, you can attach your accounts and waive normal monthly service charges!

The writer was trying to say that the CountyBank customer could request that funds in a number of deposit accounts—checking, savings, IRAs—be added together each month to show a single balance on one monthly statement. If that balance was high enough, the customer wouldn't have to pay a service charge that month. Unfortunately, the DLK got in the way of communication. So familiar to the writer was this fund-pooling arrangement that she assumed her readers were familiar with it also. Easy to see in someone else's work, hard to see in your own.

For that matter, when it comes to jargon, it's a minefield of DLK out there. Tread carefully. Jargon is insider language—shorthand that lets people in a particular field talk quickly and easily to one another—and it's incredibly useful. But it doesn't fly outside the field. Listen to the software folks discuss URIs, GUIs, and URLs—you'd think you were in a nursery, or maybe Turkey. This language is beyond many people's understanding, not because it's so difficult but simply because they haven't been exposed to it. Think about it. When you used a computer for the first time, you didn't know what an application, a spreadsheet, or default formatting was. Stock analysts had to learn the meaning of puts and calls, selling short, buying on margin, and trading commodities. Financiers weren't born knowing the terms convertible debentures and diluted equity. Doctors learned to say multi-infarct dementia and rhinitis. All these specialists are at risk of forgetting that they're using insider talk and laying it on generalists—and so are you. Because of the DLK, we forget. And of course, as surely as if we try to write Portuguese to Greeks, our communication will miscarry.

To be sure you've addressed the DLK, pretend your mother, your child, your spouse, or your carpool mate is reading what you've written. Could he or she understand it? You can even phone the person and read selected lines. (Works for me. And it gives my mother a chance to update me on her other grandchildren—the well-behaved, tidy ones.)

You can also take a cue from the *Wall Street Journal*, highly respected in business circles. It's because of the DLK that the *Wall Street Journal* never writes "IBM" without including the information that IBM is an abbreviation for International Business Machines. It usually adds a helpful identification tag line as well, such as "the computer giant"—just in case there's one person, even one, in America—I picture Rip Van Winkle waking from his 20 years' nap and reaching for the stock market page—who's unfamiliar with Big Blue. Now the *Wall Street Journal* has as well-educated and homogeneous a population as any newspaper in the country. If its writers are told to pitch, as I've heard they are, to "a bright but ignorant reader," it's surely appropriate for us to do the same. Identify; explain; describe.

Don't worry that you'll sound simplistic or condescending if you write to edit out the DLK. Business writing today is so information intensive that your readers will be happy to "cruise" past your explanation of a procedure, or definition of a word, they already know. It gives them a breather. As an editor, I notice no one's sending me a copy with a request that I make it harder to understand.

Remember also that "your reader" may include a wider audience than you imagined. So imagine this audience. Is your boss, for example, likely to pass your memo up the chain? Often the top brass are less familiar with a particular area of expertise and its jargon than you might think. They have a lot of areas to manage, and it tends to make them generalists. But because they don't like to admit that they don't understand, they feel uncomfortable, and they take it out on your copy. You don't want that. You want them to *like* what you've written.

■ **Use "I" advisedly.** Finally, and I want to go carefully here, writing for your reader means in one sense cultivating the word *you* at the expense of *I*. In one sense. I am *not* suggesting you get rid of a personal pronoun we all need and one that can add importantly to your tone. Many people writing today apparently learned from some Draconian high school teacher (when I find her, I want words with her) that *I* is always inappropriate in business writing. Good grief. As if communication weren't already impersonal enough, with printers spitting out mass mailings directed to "Customer," telephone calls reduced to a series of typing exercises on the keypad, and children linked to home only by e-mail or fiscal shortfalls. To members of a culture increasingly driven by mindless technology, *I* can come as a welcome surprise. At the very least, it means there's someone in there. So I don't want you to engage in witch-hunts against the vertical pronoun. All I want to do is raise your consciousness so you can watch for *I* as a flag that may—though it may not—signal a miscarriage of emphasis.

When you've written *I*, particularly in multiples, ask yourself whether its use is justified. Do you have a role? Why are you in there? Perhaps for a very good reason— for example, because you are responding to a letter originally written to someone else.

Dear Mr. Smith:

Thank you for taking the time to write Mr. Bergonzi, Croftman's CEO, with your suggestions for improving service to Croftman's Lynnfield customers. Mr. Bergonzi asked me to respond to your thoughtful letter, as I am the senior vice president responsible for customer relations in the Northeast Region, which includes Lynnfield.

Mr. Smith needs to know why he's hearing from you, rather than the CEO, and will be gratified that you're at a senior management level. So the information pertaining to you is relevant, and the references to yourself are appropriate.

You may also be taking it upon yourself to apologize for a glitch made by your company.

> Dear Mrs. Townsend:
>
> I apologize, on behalf of Jordan Marsh, Inc., for the inconvenience you experienced when Jordan's neglected to remove the ink cartridge from your newly purchased evening dress. I fully agree that the fault rests with the store, and we will fully compensate you for the loss of the gown. If I could compensate you for an occasion thoroughly spoiled, I would do that as well. It is unfortunate that the King of Sweden proved so aggressive in his efforts to remove the cartridge, as its explosion surely ruined the Nobel Ball for you. Again, my apologies. I have credited your account for the full price of the dress.

Note the frequency with which the personal pronoun appears in this letter. It functions here to underscore the good faith of the company toward the customer and to assure her that a sympathetic person has heard, understood, and (to the extent possible) addressed her complaint. That's a worthy *I* message.

If none of these reasons apply, you may have written an *un*worthy *I* message—one that reflects an inflated sense of self-esteem—or appears to, which is just as bad.

At the very least, though it's probably accidental, it's writer, not reader, centered. If you've identified an unworthy *I* message, see whether you can rephrase your sentence using the pronoun *you*. You get points for every *I* removed and *you* inserted.

"I" message: I hope I have explained this matter satisfactorily. If not, I'll be happy to go over it again.

"You" message: If you would like a fuller explanation, you are welcome to call me anytime at 642-7777.

The pleasant tone is there in each case, but the "you" spin brings it out.

Target your readers accurately so they'll understand what you're trying to tell them.

▨ THE BOTTOM LINE ▨

▨ **Look through your reader's eyes.**
▨ **Watch your level: how much do your readers know and understand?**
▨ **Use *I* carefully, liberally blended with *you*.**

CHAPTER 2

Have I Organized Properly?

Here's the one that drives the most bosses up the most walls. A study of Fortune 500 companies confirmed what you may have already discovered: Disorganized writing is the biggest complaint managers have about the writing of their subordinates.

We continue to focus on your audience in dealing with proper organization, which sounds hard but is really easy. To organize your writing well, all you really need to do is place the message in one of two categories: news that's *good* or *neutral* from the reader's point of view, and news that is *bad* from the reader's point of view. For good or neutral news, organize by the *Big Top* method. For bad news, use the *Rock Bottom* method.

The Big Top is the *de*ductive method of reasoning: from the major premise to the fine points. In Latin, the prefix *de-* means, among other things, "down from." This method is sometimes called the inverted pyramid: big idea on top, smaller and smaller details tapering down to the finish.

■ **The Big Top method.** This means putting your main idea first. In the first line, actually. Busy people tend not to read every word of a document. They scan. That's how President Kennedy could read an impossible number of newspapers at breakfast. (I read about this in Theodore Sorenson's biography, *Kennedy*, and lost count at 14.) What do they scan? The top line, left margin of every paragraph, that's what. Sometimes just the top line of the *first* paragraph, actually, and perhaps the last. So if you have factual or neutral news—information—make it easy for the reader to get the gist. And if you have good news—you're offering a job, awarding a contract, approving a loan—showcase it. Run it up front where the lucky reader can see it and be glad. Remember the hypothetical question: "Why this communication?" Your first sentence in such cases should answer this question.

Here's an example of an opening for a good news letter:

Dear Mrs. Shurcliff:

We agree you were overcharged for the new oil burner and installation and have enclosed a check that reflects the difference between the price we initially quoted you and the amount for which you were billed and which Mr. Shurcliff paid.

Here's another, this time the opener for a memo containing neutral news:

TO: All Regal Associates
FROM: Max Blaustein
DATE: April 24, 19___
SUBJECT: Insurance Benefit Information Session
          May 4

An all-day information session will take place in the Cronley Auditorium on May 4 from 8:00 A.M. until 5:30 P.M. Representatives of our carrier companies will speak and answer your questions. We hope everyone will be able to attend, as some of our benefit offerings have changed. Please mark the date on your calendars.

On the subject of memos, by the way, extend the Big Top principle into the heading—the subject or RE: line. Make it very descriptive, like the one above—not a title, but a headline. Not *Gone with the Wind*, in other words, but "Spirited Ante-bellum Belle Dressed in Draperies Survives War of Northern Aggression." Not *The Firm*, but "Up-and-Coming Memphis Attorney Uncovers Organized Crime Activity." You get the idea.

You can refine the Big Top method to make it easier for the reader to absorb your message. If you want to reinforce your main idea, particularly in a complex paragraph or piece, you can restate it at the end. You can also explain or amplify what you mean in the second sentence. Or you can do both. Here's a simplistic example:

Mr. Sandefur is an excellent developmental editor.	(TOPIC SENTENCE)
Rather than simply correcting errors in syntax or spelling, he revises a writer's copy so that it makes sense and is effective and pleasant to read.	(AMPLIFICATION)
He does not hesitate to tackle complex financial management reports and even technical writing. His customers over the past seven years	(SPECIFIC DETAIL SUPPORTING TOPIC SENTENCE)

include Curzon University, novelist Jane Burrows, the law firm of Polk and Maddux, and MacroFine software development. I consider him the finest developmental editor in the area.

(RESTATEMENT OF TOPIC)

The Big Top method is the way Mrs. Adams taught you to write a paragraph back in sixth grade: a topic sentence and supporting details. It works not only for a paragraph, but for a writing project as a whole.

A newspaper article is a good example of the Big Top method. The headline tells you what the entire story will be about: President Unveils Crime Plan. The rest of the article, if it's a good article, tells you what the President plans to do about crime. No more, no less. Within the article, each paragraph begins with a topic sentence that tells you what that paragraph is about: "The President outlined his plans to tackle juvenile crime . . ."; "The plan calls for $200 million to be spent . . ."; even "The President hinted at future plans to. . . ." You can scan the topic sentences and decide what you want to read about in detail.

But be careful. Faced with a blank page, especially if you're under serious time pressure (and we usually are), it's also easy to default to another mode of organizing: telling your story as it happened, from beginning to end. This is called, among other things, the chronological or lab report method. It's quick and easy writing, because it doesn't require much brainwork. All you have to do is remember the order of events and transcribe them, and you've got yourself a story. Alas, this slipshod method is usually only too evident. As Samuel Johnson wrote,

"What is written without effort is in general read without pleasure." If you use this primitive *modus operandi* for anything but a first draft, it is likely to flop.

Here, for example, is a paragraph that tracks events chronologically:

> On January 2, John was given the task of developing the fiscal-year business plan for Amtex. After working on it for two months, he presented it at the Amtex board meeting in March. The chairman of the board and various members asked a number of questions about cost, time frame, and management realignments, which he was able to answer to their satisfaction. Ultimately, the board unanimously approved the plan, effective immediately.

Well, the author walked us right through John's story from the beginning to the end, and what a dull, dumb story it was. Why is it so dumb and dull? Because priority has been assigned solely on the basis of *when* things happened, not on their relative importance. The reader must wait till the last sentence before the really significant information, the approval of the plan, emerges. The walk-through works well with stories that begin "Once upon a time," but you're not the Brothers Grimm, nor are you dealing with that level of reader involvement. Rather than waiting with bated breath for you to come to the point, your readers may simply stop reading. Why not? They can't see what you're driving at. Or whether you're driving at anything.

In these latter days of shortened sound bites and diminishing attention spans, the prize goes to the person who spits the message out first. So if you've got something to say, say it. Jam the essentials into the first line, right up against the left-hand margin. In most cases, this means ignoring chronology and leading instead with what is actually in most cases the conclusion, or the result. In your end is your beginning, as it were, like that snake with its tail in its mouth.

Here's the paragraph on John's business plan, reorganized on the Big Top principle:

> We will implement John's business plan immediately, after its approval yesterday by unanimous vote of the Amtex board of directors. The weeks of work he has put into the plan since he was given this responsibility January 2 paid off. He was able to answer the board's intensive questioning into the plan's provisions for cost, time frame, and management realignments to everyone's satisfaction.

Sometimes you may be asked to use the chronological method—for an update, for example. This doesn't prevent your inserting a two- or three-line recommendation or summary at the top. This effectively turns the piece into a Big Top document.

One writing student told me he didn't like to reveal his message deductively. He preferred to create suspense, he told me, ignoring the cynicism deepening in my face. He aspired to lead his readers along as he spun a web. Or something. Please, please believe me, this technique will not work. In fact, it's a route to self-destruction as a communicator. You are not writing a mystery novel, nor doing the Dance of the Seven Veils. Put your readers in the picture right away.

Now that I've told you how ineffective this method is for good or neutral news, let me show you how well it works for *bad* news.

■ **The Rock Bottom method.** When you have to communicate bad news, you organize *in*ductively, which in Latin literally means "leading in." You begin with the details and work toward the conclusion. Rather than being positioned up front for maximum exposure, your message doesn't appear until the end of the paragraph or piece. Here's an example of a paragraph that's organized on the Rock Bottom principle:

> Your performance during the past six months has been erratic. In fact, our clients have found it difficult even to reach you, and that is understandable, as your schedule shows a record of absenteeism for a variety of reasons, none of them related to work. In addition, the documents you were charged with preparing either have not been completed or show evidence of having been hastily and sloppily prepared. In view of these facts, I feel I have no choice but to place you on probationary status until your work improves.

Despite its chronological relating of events—from the start of the six months to the present—this paragraph is ideally organized, because the message is a negative one. The payoff is bad news. And for bad news we use the message-last approach. It's sometimes called the pyramid method: working from the little stuff to the big stuff. I call it Rock Bottom, picturing the reader receiving the bad news—the refusal, the summons, the chop—and feeling that this apocryphal location has been hit.

The advantages of the Rock Bottom method for conveying bad news are threefold. First, you **cushion the blow** by leading up to it. Consider a bad-news message such as this one, wrongly organized by the Big Top method:

> We can't let you go to the conference in Winchester. Senior staff met yesterday and decided you shouldn't go for the following reasons. First . . .

Right up front with the bad news. This is rude, and it's insensitive. It's almost as if the writer enjoys being a bad hat. Not a good message to send to subordinates, or anyone else. In contrast, the inductive method, because it's indirect, can make you seem perhaps just a shade unwilling to break the news.

Second, you **build a case.** By the time your reader reaches the unwelcome conclusion, he or she at least understands why you came to it. You make your plea for the inevitability of the final blow.

Third, you **ensure you're heard**. If you slug the reader with your ugly message up front, he or she may well read no further. That's the way many people react to bad news. If you want to be certain your entire message is read, you'd better Rock Bottom it.

Finally, a few quick tricks for organizing that will improve any piece:

■ **Use "connective tissue" to show the direction of your thinking.** We all want to omit needless words, but certain words are critical to your meaning. Don't omit words such as *in addition, however, although,* and *but.* These words are not there just to connect gracefully. They perform an essential function in showing your reader the relationship between what you've just said and what you're about to say. The Dangerous Level of Knowledge (DLK) sometimes makes us think we don't need these words. That's only because we already know the story. The reader needs them a lot. Consider:

> John says he thinks a takeover is highly unlikely.
> He is preparing a "poison pill" clause to help us protect ourselves in a takeover situation.

Without the magic word *although, but,* or *however,* these two sentences make no sense together. They contradict each other. I won't belabor the obvious. Be free with your connective tissue: it helps your reader follow the direction of your thinking. *However* prepares the brain for a contradiction. For readers who weren't paying close attention, it's also a signal to go back and make sure they know what's about to be contradicted.

Again because of the Dangerous Level of Knowledge, I'm strongly inclined to let my structure— the "bones," or underlying organizational principles— show. Consequently, I love words such as *first, second,* and *third;* and phrases such as *in the past, in the present,* and *in the future.* These not only show readers what you're driving at, but they also bring careless ones up short—if they arrive at *third,* for example, and realize they've already missed two points.

These words are powerful rhetorical devices that keep the reader abreast of your thinking.

■ **Be true to your contract with the reader.** If you plan to discuss several items, list them in an order that you like. Then **follow that order**. Don't cite items 1, 2, and 3, then go on to discuss item 3 first. This is breaking an implied deal you've made with the reader. Let's say you're going to write about housing in the city, the suburbs, and rural areas. You craft a topic sentence that reads just about like that. Now that you've so ordered them, you are bound to discuss the city first. (If you decide you'd rather talk about the suburbs first, reorder your topic sentence and start with the suburbs.)

▪ **Work from the easy to the difficult.** Follow this rule in a series of words or phrases, unless some other organizing principle is in effect:

> Your office furniture will include a desk, a credenza, and three five-drawer file cabinets.

The nature of the brain, to my limited understanding, is such that it appreciates receiving the simple item first, which "primes" it to understand the function of the more complex ones that follow. Makes sense to me, and it sounds good too: Mairzy doats, and doazy doats, and little lambsy divey. Fish nor fowl nor good red herring. Gold, and myrrh, and frankincense. The Niña, the Pinta, and the Santa María. You get the idea.

▪ **Use bullets and numbering to clarify points.** Remember, numbering gives you two benefits that bullets don't: You set priorities with numbers, and you can identify a numbered item for reference. It's easy to refer to number 6, rather than to "the next-to-last, I'm sorry, next-to-*next-to*-last bullet."

Sound easy? It is.

▧ THE BOTTOM LINE ▧

- Use the Big Top method (major point first) for good or neutral news.
- Use the Rock Bottom method (major point last) for bad news.
- Show the direction of your thinking with connective tissue: *however, therefore*.
- Discuss points in the same order in which you introduce them: 1, 2, 3.
- Work from the easy to the difficult when listing a series of items.
- Use bullets and numbering for clarity.

CHAPTER 3

Have I Used a Tone That Will Appeal to My Reader?

The tone of a piece of writing is its overall mood: the writer's attitude toward the material and toward the reader. And it is extremely important. Remember "Don't look at me in that tone of voice!"? Tone is the key to your salability. It can help you convince the skeptical, pacify the irate, stroke the philanthropic, rally the uncommitted. By the same token, if you don't have tone elements under control, you can alienate your readers.

The following rules will help you edit out tones that alienate. From time to time you may need to use them to punish a sinner or whatever: my aim here is to make sure you realize when you're doing that, and aren't just whacking away undoing people unaware. Because it infuses your entire message, tone is a powerful tool.

Here are some quick and easy ways to ensure a winning tone:

■ **Edit out a negative point of view.** Most of us are problem solvers. Therefore, it's easy for us to fall into the trap of writing about what's wrong, what we can't promise, can't do, can't get. Most of the time, this is not a desirable tone. It's easy to spot negative writing, once you're reminded. It tends, not surprisingly, to have a lot of negative words in it: words like *unfortunately, no, not, unable, impossible,* and anything that ends in *n't.* These are all words to edit out if you want a positive tone. *Fail, regret,* and *disappointment* are also near the top of my hit list.

Luckily, most negative writing can easily be recast in a positive form. If your work is stressing what isn't doable, try thinking positively and stressing what is:

Negative: Our company does not deal with the public.
Positive: Our company deals exclusively with distributors.

Negative: We can't let you use the equipment on weekends.
Positive: Feel free to use the equipment any weekday.

Negative: We regret to inform you that you are currently ineligible for benefits.
Positive: When you complete a waiting period, you'll be eligible for benefits.

It's like thinking of your caffe latte cup as half full rather than half empty.

■ **Edit out tentative writing.** Your reader seeks to learn from you. As a writer, you represent, in a sense, authority. If you couch your message in uncertain or shilly-shallying language, he or she may question whether you can be believed and trusted. Unless you have a particular reason to sound unsure of yourself, don't fall into these traps and lose reader confidence.

1. Using tentative verb forms. *Would, should,* and *could* are conditionals that can make you sound unsure how your information will be received.

    No: If our proposal is accepted, we *would* implement a full-scale waterproofing of the dome.

    Yes: If our proposal is accepted, we *will* implement. . . . (Or, thinking positively, *When* our . . .)

    The same goes for the *-ing* verb form, or present participle. Use it sparingly and advisedly. There's a big difference in tone between the following two sentences:

    I *am expecting* your draft by tomorrow.
    I *expect* your draft by tomorrow.

    On occasion, you may prefer the softer tone of the first, but be aware that's the tone *-ing* creates.

2. Littering your writing with qualifiers. Sometimes you have to. But when you sprinkle your writing with *a bit, rather, somewhat, to a certain degree,* and so forth, you appear to be sitting on the fence, hedging your bets, and covering your you-know-what. All this silly activity causes readers to lose faith, and who can blame them? For example:

    I am somewhat in favor of selling a little of the company's stock.

Well, are you or aren't you? You owe your reader, if possible, an unequivocal answer.

I believe it will benefit us to sell between 10,000 and 40,000 shares of company stock.

I'd like to point out one other aspect of this modifying business. If you modify strong adjectives, those descriptive words, you will come off sounding eccentric, or worse: to the extent the adjective is powerful in its own right, you will make yourself—I have to say it—ridiculous. I had a friend who used to insist on saying things were "very terrible." (Making matters worse, she was from a rural hamlet of southwest Virginia, and she pronounced it something like "vurry turrible.") I couldn't persuade her not to say it, but I think I finally convinced her not to put it in writing. Here's an example in print from a company president and CEO:

> When [Phil] was talking to the board yesterday, he showed the market to book, which is a *relatively critical* number, and which is now hovering at 300 percent. . . .

Either something's critical or it isn't. The stronger the descriptive word, the more foolish you appear when you modify it. Our CEO could have omitted *relatively* with no damage to his message. Similar words that I believe should never be modified include (there are plenty more, but you'll get the idea):

changeless	ironclad
correct	omnipotent
immovable	pregnant
immutable	unique

So be careful with the modifiers. Don't compromise strong words with modifiers that weaken them and make you look silly.

■ **Edit out any suggestion of manipulation.** Two maneuvers to avoid so you don't appear to be turning on an artificial brand of charm to get your way. (You can certainly do that, but I don't want you to get caught doing it, and some moves are just too obvious.)

First, don't thank anyone in advance. It's hypocritical—how can you be grateful for something that hasn't taken place? It also indicates that you are quite sure your wishes will be followed, so it preempts free will on the reader's part.

> So that we may share our findings with the Board of Directors at the Annual Meeting, please have 20 copies of the satisfaction survey on my desk by 5:00 P.M. Thank you in advance for your attention to this matter.

Right. And you're not welcome.

Second, don't keep using the reader's name in an e-mail, memo, or letter.

This ploy is intensely easy to overdo. And, partly because it's been overdone, a lot of people really don't like it, I among them. As a bond trader friend of mine who spends a lot of time with salesmen says, "I can't stand to hear the sound of my own name ringing in my ears." It's pretty much the same in writing—except that in a face-to-face conversation the twitch of annoyance across your reader's features will tell you you are overdoing it. It's bad enough in a one-off personal communication; it's even worse, I think, in a direct-mail piece, because everyone knows the names are input by braindead keypunch operators and spat out by computers:

> Bucky Bueckberger, you may have ALREADY won $1 million!!!!

(Now why would I be suspicious of such a charming message?)

In primitive cultures, to know someone's name is to have the power of life and death over the person; therefore one's real name is a jealously guarded secret. Even in modern civilization, people's names are still essential parts of their being. So be careful how you toss a person's name around in your communications. To you it may appear a harmless stratagem, friendly and personal, but it can be perceived as an irritating, even controlling, maneuver by your reader. If you're still convinced namedropping will charm someone, go ahead, but at least limit yourself to one drop per communication.

■ **Edit out *unintentional* unkindness.** Occasionally a piece of writing must be harsh or unpleasant in tone. But too often people surprise me by writing—to an audience of customers, for example—in an appallingly unkind way. There's rarely an upside to writing unpleasantly to somebody up the chain from you, as customers are by definition. When challenged, my cruel and unusual writers are often amazed. They had no idea how they were coming across. A few suggestions to avoid writing that's unintentionally rough on your readers:

1. Watch generalizations that put people or groups down, directly or indirectly.

   MIT students are poor conversationalists outside their own fields of expertise.

   Wellesley women make good lawyers.

   That second sentence will offend alumnae from six out of the former seven sister colleges, and any number of lawyers—many more than the Wellesley alumnae it will flatter. That's not even good business economics.

2. Edit out language that blames or belittles.

   If you had read the manual we sent with your laser printer, you would not be experiencing a problem with sheet slippage.

   As you are surely aware, this seminar is available to corporate clients only.

   Most people realize that ABC is a closely held corporation.

3. Ditto language that patronizes or self-applauds at readers' expense.

   We have a lot of experience helping people who can't grasp the basics of math.

A prestigious law firm such as Grad, Levy naturally receives many requests like yours.

Kindly send us a copy of your certification as a harbor pilot.

(If ever a word had overtones that belie its sound, the word is *kindly,* in the sense used above—sort of a one-word oxymoron. I never, ever use it.)

4. Check to be sure you haven't unwittingly expressed disbelief.

If, as you say, your contract stipulates services through the end of this year . . .

You seem to be suggesting that it is we who owe you money.

You claim that we sent your package on April 8.

Such sentences are necessary and appropriate on certain occasions—shortly before you go to court, perhaps. But the old definition of a gentleman is "One who never inflicts pain unintentionally." Don't inflict pain by mistake in your writing. Strive to be a person of gentility, as we say in these politically correct days (see Chapter 14).

■ **Remove strained, overly formal, or outdated language.** Relax already. Queen Victoria is no longer with us, and flowery phrases have abdicated in favor of conversational language. (I said conversational, not colloquial. Your business writing needs to be able to pass the read-aloud test, but it shouldn't sound as if you're talking with your best friend. At least not the one who taught you to swear.) This means you can dispense with

> Enclosed please find
> Hoping to hear from you, I remain
> I beg to remind you
> We deem it necessary
> As of even date herewith
> Pursuant to
> Inasmuch as
> Yours of the first inst. (whatever that is)

and similarly labored phrases. Pleading, begging, and deeming are out, presumably for the count: try asking, suggesting, and believing.

■ **When you must apologize, do it up front and in full.** If, I mean when, you or your organization goofs—it's going to happen—admit it and say you're sorry, rather than trying to protect yourself. The latter builds a defensive wall between you and the reader. Besides, it lacks style. As somebody said about slipping on the ice, it's not the falling down that looks so bad, it's the effort to stay upright. Trying not to apologize is much the same. It's not only ungraceful, though—it also isn't fair. If you owe, you should pay up. Besides, it's hard to stay mad with someone who is figuratively rolling over and putting four paws in the air. So apologize at the beginning of your message. Apologize profusely. If you have a rebate, or premium, or little present you can throw in, or a pile of money (mends many fences) go ahead and do that too— just be sure your organization will back you up.

No: Evidently a mistake was made somewhere along the line. Two's Company regrets the occurrence. Complaints about our service are infrequent . . .

Yes: On behalf of Two's Company, I apologize for the error in your March billing and the inconvenience you experienced as a result. At Two's we try very hard to prevent such mistakes. Occasionally, they nonetheless do occur. We have credited your account with the amount of the overcharge . . .

▪ **If someone *else* goofed, don't whine about it.** Sometimes it's not your fault, it's the other guys'. Give them a break. It could have been you: we all make mistakes. Simply state the facts and ask for whatever apology or reparation you need. Don't drone on and on about how awful it was for you. Nobody likes a whiner, and nobody likes a martyr. Remember the parental lament, "After all I've done for you, this is the thanks I get?" Did it make you sorry, or just plain mad? Why compromise your relationship with the goofer? That only adds to the problem.

Here are two letters dealing with the same issue: a business broker has been referring inappropriate prospects as buyers for the writer's company. The first letter is subjective and emotional; the second, objective and factual.

Dear Steve:

Last week you showed my company to yet another window shopper who has neither the collateral to obtain financing nor any in-depth understanding of what it takes to run a business such as Wyziwhiz Works. In fact, I don't think Jack Smith understands what a printed circuit board is, let alone the complex issues involved in estimating a job, making the parts, assembling them, and getting them to the customer in a timely manner. You are taking up my time, of which I have so little nowadays, and with each person you bring in to see me, you are increasing my risk of losing my best employees if word that I am seeking a buyer should get out.

I am tired of your cavalier attitude toward the suitability of the potential buyers you bring in here. You seem to think I have nothing better to do with my time than conduct pointless interviews. Frankly, considering the enormous fees you charge and my questionable return on investment, I think I'm entitled to be angry and frustrated, and I am.

Steve, I have been running this company for 30 years. Perhaps you can imagine my feeling for an enterprise in which I've invested so much time and energy. It's incredibly hard for me even to contemplate turning it over to anyone else, unless one of my children is interested, which seems unlikely. But I feel especially betrayed by your dragging in as prospective buyers people who are utterly unqualified. It's not appropriate, and it's not fair. Just wanted you to know how I feel.

Sincerely,

Well, he makes it clear how he feels, all right. He's raised whining to an art form. Look at the emotionally charged language he uses: *entitled, angry and frustrated, betrayed, not fair.* Words like these should be used sparingly and advisedly in business writing, not piled on top of one another. He's also dragged in a lot of irrelevant material: a walk-through of what his job entails, the demands on his time, his children's lack of interest in the business.

If you can't write objectively because you're angry or feeling ill used, it's probably better to wait awhile and gain some perspective. Or dash off the furious letter and stick it in a drawer somewhere until you're calm. Then throw it away. Here's the second letter:

Dear Steve:

I enjoyed chatting with Jack Smith yesterday. It seems clear, however, that his work as a technician and his lack of financial assets qualify him poorly to purchase Wyziwhiz Works. The same is true of the last three prospects I have met through you.

Wyziwhiz Works has increased sales by over 23 percent in the past four months, so I am very busy. I am also deeply concerned that word of my intent to sell the company may leak out. You'll recall that two years ago a prospective buyer discussed my plans with an employee, and as a direct result both my sales vice president and my general manager left me for more secure positions.

Bearing these facts in mind, as well as the considerable amount I've invested in your brokerage operation, I ask that you screen prospects most

carefully in the future. I appreciate your attention
to this matter.

Sincerely,

This writer basically has a grip. Rather than calling
attention to his feelings, he cites facts to reinforce his
points. He sticks to the subject. As a bonus, this letter is
half the length of the first. Which one would you rather
receive? Don't boycott gripes altogether: a tone of
healthy anger may well be justified. I just want to point
out that the primary reward for complaining at length is
hostility.

■ **If you must be funny, be very, very careful.** I
absolutely hate to say that—there's too little humor in the
world as it is, particularly in the black-and-white world of
business—but I have to warn you to watch out. A writing
teacher of mine once said, where business writing is concerned, "Humor doesn't travel well." Sadly, I have to agree.
My suggestion is to limit your repartee to face-to-face or
telephone encounters. Why? For two major reasons.

First, your humor may not be taken as it was intended.
In most cases, the people you're writing to aren't close
friends. They may misunderstand, take offense, even be
hurt. And with writing you don't get a second chance. If
in a conversation your witty remark is greeted with
aggrieved or affronted silence, you have an opportunity
to redeem yourself: you can explain what you meant, or
apologize, or offer to send an attractive gift . . . With writing, you don't have that luxury. The words sit there on the
page, continuing to reverberate, documenting for all time
your failure to amuse.

Well, maybe it isn't usually that bad. But it is risky.

Second, your piece may be read by someone other than the person for whom you originally wrote it. You run the risk of appearing obscure or bizarre to this secondary audience. This applies to the copy in the file also. Think about whether you want your clever sallies to surface five years from now and be read by uncomprehending, unappreciative strangers. And it applies to e-mail in spades.

E-mail, by its nature, is casual and informal. But *it isn't private,* and don't you forget it. If your company wants to read your e-mail, the system allows for this. Even without senior management hacking into your e-mail correspondence and failing to chuckle, think very hard about whether you'd be comfortable if someone copied your e-mail, complete with witticisms, to your group or to a wider audience. People can be surprisingly thoughtless about doing so. If they want to add a comment on the substance of your message and share it around the department, they may not reread to see whether remarks contained in your original message could backfire—and sometimes they do. You've probably already been warned about the hazards of forgetting that your e-mail is *about* a person, inadvertently hitting a button, and sending it *to* the person. Stories circulate about that clumsy maneuver that could freeze your blood.

Yes, once in a while someone goes for the jocular vein in print and gets away with it. My friend Arthur runs a summer program for elementary school children. His direct-mail campaign each spring consists of one letter, which begins with a cheery salutation along the lines of *"Helloooo, fellow campers! George of the Jungle here!"* (Emphasis Arthur's.) People who aren't familiar with

Arthur are mystified or scared. Luckily, Arthur's program is so terrific it doesn't matter: the moms who know clue in those who don't. So Arthur doesn't really care what people think of his letters, or his sense of humor. He just goes on expressing himself. But that's a luxury most of us can't afford.

In conclusion, be attentive to these seven issues of tone, even if you don't happen to be feeling all the right feelings toward your audience. As Lady Macbeth used to tell her spouse, "Assume a virtue if you have it not." You'll convince readers that you are kind, trustworthy, sensitive, and on their side—combining, in fact, the best features of the Boy Scouts and I'm OK You're OK therapy.

▨ THE BOTTOM LINE ▨

- **Write positively, not negatively.**
- **Write surely, not tentatively.**
- **Don't manipulate your readers, at least not overtly.**
- **Remove stiff or dated language.**
- **Apologize immediately and completely.**
- **Don't whine on and on about someone's mistake.**
- **Handle humor cautiously, if at all.**

CHAPTER 4

Have I Preferred Active to Passive Verbs?

Your boss may return a piece of writing to you for revision with comments such as "You need to zero in on the concept—tighten it up" or "It seems sort of vague—kind of wordy, too." Such remarks aren't specific enough to be helpful. That's frustrating for you. Remember, however, that it's frustrating for your boss as well. While I can't say for sure what you may be doing wrong, it's a good guess that part of your problem is an over-reliance on passive verb constructions. And though people often can't put their finger on just what's the matter with writing that's passive-intensive, they know they don't like it.

If you've never thought about the difference between active and passive verb forms, it's time you did. The active, or *to do,* form of a verb is simply a past, present, or future verb, usually paired with a subject, and looking more or less like these examples:

I *led*	we *have accomplished*
he *says*	you *will send*

A passive, or *to be done,* verb form is the past tense of a verb—*led, accomplished, said, sent*—with any form of the verb *to be:*

I *was led*	the job *was accomplished*
it *will be said*	the letter *has been sent*

I will get out on my customary limb and say that the passive is an inferior, clumsy verb form. Nine times out of ten you don't need it and shouldn't use it. Having said so, I'll take three minutes to show you three uses for it. If you can't show you're using the passive voice for one of these three reasons, you should cut it from your piece without mercy.

▪ **Use the passive voice in three situations.** I won't deny it: passive verbs can be useful. You can use them

1. When you don't know who did something:

    The gun *was fired* at close range.

2. To protect a person or organization:

    A mistake *was made* in Customer Service. On behalf of Acme, I apologize for any inconvenience.

    (It was Betsy's first day on the job: let's give her another chance. If this customer gets her name, she's toast.)

3. Occasionally, if the object of your sentence is much more the news or the point:

    President Reagan *was shot* on his way to the Capitol steps.

> The final draft *was collated, addressed,* and *mailed* in less than four hours.

Readers may care considerably less who shot: the president is the focus of attention. And they may not care at all, depending on the context, what exhausted persons collated, addressed, and mailed. In fact, if different persons performed the operations, the sentence would become impossibly unwieldy:

> In less than four hours, Michele collated the final draft, Duane addressed the envelopes, and Jason took all the copies to the mailbox.

The only possible justification for such writing is that you are showcasing the stars of your organization and how hard they work. *Do not* take Rule 3 as a license to start using the passive voice indiscriminately. You want to watch out for overworking the form. *The passive voice can run you into trouble if you use it as a default on ordinary occasions.*

■ **Prefer the active mode in virtually every other situation.** Overuse of the passive voice is an unwholesome habit. What's wrong with it? A couple of things.

> *It was decided* to shift the report deadline to April 2.
> John *was expected* to present the report today.
> The PC *was removed* last week.

It's a strength of this voice that, in these examples as in those preceding, it allows you to omit the initiator of the action from the sentence. Yet, paradoxically, it can also be a serious weakness. Dropping the prime mover and shaker from your sentence **can make you look bad**: evasive, shifty, possibly trying to avoid blame.

> Your tax records seem *to have been mislaid.*

Or timid, or poorly informed, or vague, or stupid. Hm. I'm beginning to wonder whether it's worth it.

And that's not all. If you do include the perpetrator, it **always takes more words** to write in the passive:

> Active: The accountant *cooked* the books.
> Passive: The books *were cooked* by the accountant.

Why take up space with needless words? And these are those words.

Last, the passive voice **inverts and subverts action**. Since written English runs from left to right, the action of a sentence typically takes the same route. In an archetypal active sentence, a *subject* does an *action* to an *object.* For example:

> ➤ ➤ ➤ ➤
> (left to right): The accountant *cooked* the books.

The structure of a passive sentence, however, runs counter to expectation, i.e., from right to left.

> ◄ ◄ ◄ ◄
> (right to left): The books *were cooked* by the accountant.

All right, so it's not exactly flying in the face of nature. It's still a little odd. And the inversion can make the writing seem static, action poor.

Give yourself points for every unnecessary passive verb you rewrite in the active mode. If you're being honest, you'll see that few of them are really justified:

Passive: The minutes *were read* by the secretary.
Active: The secretary *read* the minutes.

You may have to do some work if you've used a passive verb to hide the fact that you don't know something you should:

Passive: The prize *will be presented* at tomorrow's
         department meeting.
         (If you have no idea who's handing it out,
         it's definitely time to inquire.)

Active: President and CEO John Allen *will present* the prize at . . .
         (Incontestably a better line overall.)

Sometimes you can simply choose a different verb:

Passive: Passengers *were awarded* 500 bonus
         miles for the flight.
Active: Passengers *received* 500 bonus miles for
         the flight.

To help you spot passive verbs, look for *to be* in any of its forms—*will have been* seen, *was* expected, *was to have been* given. It can be a clue that passives have crept into your writing, generally to its disadvantage.

▥ THE BOTTOM LINE ▥

▤ **Choose passive verbs only if**
> **the doer of the action is unknown**
> **you want to protect the doer**
> **the object of action is the point rather than the doer**

▤ **Remember that passive verbs can**
> **make you look shifty or evasive**
> **make your sentence wordy**
> **cause the action of the sentence to run in reverse**

CHAPTER 5

Have I Used the Right Word?

C hoosing and using words correctly will raise your score with your boss and your readers. It's a pleasure when a writer drops in the *mot juste*, or just-right word (well, maybe not your idea of pleasure, but discriminating readers enjoy it, and we aim to please). By the same token, use of the wrong word will significantly undermine the confidence of a fastidious reader, which no one can afford to do. And your spell checker blithely passes on the misuse of words. Here are assorted pairs and snares that can trip business writers, causing them to convey an unintended image to their readers—an unfortunate subtext that makes them appear to be in poor control of their material.

I have listed below four categories of words that cause trouble: confused, misused, abused, and not to be used. Please pay close attention if people have accused you of malapropisms (after Mrs. Malaprop, the Dickens heroine guilty of committing "putrefied with fear" and other linguistic enormities) or if you yourself suspect your word choices are sometimes a few degrees off.

Confused. In this category are words that look or sound alike. In business writing, the most familiar pairs include the following. If you don't want to have to keep referring to the list, I've added some memory boosters you may find helpful.

averse: adj. against or unwilling: " I am *averse* to the idea of a merger."

adverse   adj. unfavorable: "Don't risk an *adverse* credit rating."

affect: v. to have an impact on; n: capacity for emotional response

effect: v. to bring about: "*effect* a change"; n: result: "the *effect* of the restructuring"

Remember: The two most useful senses of each word are alphabetical. First, you *a*ffect something or someone; then you see the *e*ffect. *Affect* as a noun is unlikely to be part of business writing. As for *effect* as a verb, you're on your own.

any time   whenever: "*any time* you're feeling blue"

anytime   at any time whatsoever: "Call us *anytime,* day or night"

capital   available cash; town or city that is seat of government

capitol   the building where state legislature meets

Capitol   Washington, D.C., building where U.S. Congress meets

compare to   to suggest a similarity: "He compared me *to* James Reston."

compare
with

to make an examination of two things, addressing their differences and similarities: "We compared the figures *with* those of the preceding quarter."

Remember: In business writing, you're almost always comparing *with*. Comparing *to* is more frequent in literature: "Shall I compare thee to a summer's day?"

complement to form a valuable part of, to add to in a positive way

compliment to praise or pay a compliment to

Remember: *Complement* is probably the word you want; it's generally the more useful in a business context. To me, the first five letters of the word look like the word "couple," which is what complementing is—a productive joining of two parts.

continual again and again: "*continual* objections from the Senate floor"

continuous uninterrupted: "a *continuous* flow of new business"

Remember: The last three letters of continu*ous* stand for "one uninterrupted sequence." (I wish I'd thought that up.)

council governing body
counsel lawyer, advice; to advise

ensure to guarantee
insure to cover by selling or purchasing insurance

Remember: *in*sure with *in*surance. Although most dictionaries allow you to use *insure* for both meanings, this distinction is one many insurance companies themselves prefer to make. You won't offend anyone by making it, but you might offend someone if you don't.

farther	a greater distance
further	in greater depth, more

Remember: f*a*rther refers to *a*ctual distance.

flounder	to struggle, thrash about in confusion
founder	to fail utterly, sink to the bottom

Remember: The *l* in f*l*ounder stands for life, and while there's life there's hope. For a *foundering* enterprise, there is no hope. It has collapsed down to its origins, or *foundations.*

pedal	v. to propel, as a bicycle, by the act of moving pedals
peddle	v. to sell, or attempt to sell

If it weren't for influence peddling, we wouldn't need this in a business writing book. Unfortunately, these two words sound exactly alike, but they don't share any element of meaning. The word you're likely to want is *peddle,* a complimentary synonym for *sell.*

principal	n. capital as opposed to interest; important person; adj: main, primary
principle	n. basic truth, rule, or policy

Remember: Not hard if you bear in mind that *principle* is a noun with just one meaning: a basic truth, tenet, etc. Everything else, noun or adjective, is *principal.*

saving	a reduction in cost or expense
savings	the plural form of saving, with the same meaning

You can realize *a saving* or *savings,* e.g., if you shop at Walmart, but you cannot realize *a savings.* It's just as incorrect as writing *a briefcases* or *a meetings.* It just happens to be more common. I hadn't paid much attention to the issue until a senior executive noted how much she disliked *a savings* in the advertising her company was doing. In fact, she was taking it out of copy and giving the advertising agency a piece of her mind every time she found it. The *American Heritage Dictionary* Usage Panel (more about the this group in Chapter 11) is with her on this one: 57 percent found the phrase unacceptable. Says the panel in one of its many interesting Usage Notes: "*a saving* is the only uncontroversial form."

Think no one will notice if you're a letter or two off? Here's a story just for you. I once got a call the night before Thanksgiving from a friend, an advertising copy writer, who seemed oddly insistent that I okay "We'll help compl*i*ment your needs."

"It's sort of like being polite to them, right?" said Kevin. "Paying them a compliment?"

"Of course it isn't," I answered. "Tell me you didn't."

"I did," he admitted. On two thousand brochures. Instead of perfecting his pecan pie recipe, he spent the night gluing two thousand tiny little *e*'s on top of *i*'s because his boss was so furious she refused to pay for a reprint. This didn't have to happen. Make sure it doesn't happen to you.

■ **Misused.** This category includes pairs that are wrongly thought to be interchangeable. It also includes words that many business writers use incorrectly.

amount,
number
They are different, but it's easy to know which to use. Write *number,* not *amount,* for things you can count. It's therefore "the *number* of pennies," but "the *amount* of cash."

ambiguous unclear in meaning
ambivalent uncertain in one's feelings

Again, the alphabet helps out here. First comes the unclear item, which is ambiguous; then follows the reaction, which is ambivalent.

among amid more than two: "You're *among* friends."
between usually said of two things: "We must choose *between* two strategies."

However, consider "talks between Germany, France, and Italy" or "Relations between Jane and her two assistants have never been good." *Among* doesn't sound right in these sentences. Some people suggest that when the action is going between all possible twosomes (Germany and France, Germany and Italy, France and Italy), the proper choice is *between.* Others simply say the distinction is not all that clear. You can let your ear be your guide, or you can rephrase your sentence: "Jane has never gotten along with her two assistants."

bring to carry (literally or figuratively) toward
take to carry (literally or figuratively) away

I've seen this distinction in almost every manual I've ever read, so somebody must be misusing these words. If you've been doing it, stop it. We're not going to waste any more of our time on it.

comprise   to include
compose   to make up

Remember my suggestion that you write defensively? *Comprise* is often used nowadays as a synonym for *compose,* as in "The board is comprised of six members," and it bothers some people. I get to hear about it. (Get into this business and such people will pick on you at parties as though you were personally responsible.) Although this meaning has now achieved dictionary status, a number of well-educated people prefer the original meaning, roughly synonymous with "embrace." Why risk annoying anyone? No one will notice if you *don't* use *comprise* in its nouveau sense. Here's how to please everyone:

> The board *comprises* six members.
> The board *is composed of* representatives from each region.

enormity   In its most precise sense refers to awfulness, rather than size. "The *enormity* of his crime overwhelmed him."

evoke   to call forth
invoke   to call upon

Remember your Latin: the meanings are direct translations. If time and trouble have wiped Latin from your memory, go with *evoke,* which is what we usually try to do with a response. *Invoke* may involve calling on the spirits of ancestors, gods, former bosses, etc., thus tending to be a little poetic for business writing. But it is useful when someone calls on a law or principle, such as client-customer privilege.

The drop in the Dow *evoked* mass selloffs.
The plaintiff *invoked* the Fifth Amendment.

fewer, less   Like *amount* and *number.* If you can't separate and count the items under discussion, write *less:* "*Less* disturbance in the bond market." If you can count them, it's *fewer:* "We hired *fewer* employees than last year."

fulsome   offensively insincere. When you offer fulsome praise, you are not, as some people think, praising something in the fullest sense. You are in fact praising hypocritically; you are overdoing it (i.e., you are full of it).

i.e.   that is, in other words. From Latin *id est*
e.g.   for example. From Latin *exempli gratia*

imply   to suggest without openly stating
infer   to gather from something said or written

These are easy to distinguish, although too many people don't. The chronology is alphabetical: you have to *imply* something before anything can be *inferred.*

individual   Avoid using this word as a synonym for *person:* "I've asked two *individuals* to handle this project." Use it as a noun only if you are distinguishing a person from a group: "One *individual* stands out in this department."

lay   to put or place; past is *laid*
lie   to recline; past is *lay*

Let's *lay* this error to rest. I will no longer take it *lying* down.

like   Don't use *like* as a synonym for *as if, such as,* or *as.* If you've written a *like* you think is suspect, try substituting each of the three:

> He looks *like* he needs a break. (Only *as if* works.)
> We need a motto, *like* "Excelsior." (*Such as* makes sense, sounds good.)
> He is a hard worker, *like* you said. (It should be *as.*)

Some people have trouble differentiating between *like* and *as* in a sentence such as that last one. You should find it easy if you remember that *like* precedes a noun and *as* precedes a verb:

> If it walks *like* a duck, quacks *like* a duck . . .
> Just *as* I said, just *as* I am . . .

literally   in a literal, or by-the-book, sense: really and truly
figuratively in a metaphorical sense; *not* really or truly

For heaven's sake, don't misuse these. Your reader will think you are a figurative dodo. Even in conversation, you crash and burn with a line such as "I was literally dead on my feet." Your listeners will be looking for signs of necrosis. Get a grip: you were *figuratively* dead. Employing *literally* as an all-purpose intensifier suggests that you think the almost-right word will do. Or that you are clueless.

may   refers to future activity in a present-tense context
might   refers to future activity in a past-tense context

> He says he *may* join Arnold Advisory Services.
> He said he *might* join Arnold Advisory Services.

It's as simple as that—with, this being English, the usual additional quirk: to indicate a significant shade of doubt, use *might* in the present context: "He *might* join us, although his train doesn't get in until 5:00."

noisome   means obnoxious, odorous, or toxic; not a synonym for *noisy*

select: adj. special, exclusive: "a *select* group of investors"

selected: adj. chosen from a group: "*selected* items are on sale"

There's an overlap of meaning—both adjectives imply a process of selection—but only in the first case is superiority the criterion for being chosen. We may or may not know why the *selected* items were selected.

shall, will   Why bother with *shall* when you can use *will?* At best, you're dealing with a verb form that's increasingly rare; at worst, you'll come across as affected. Leave *shall* to the writers of contracts.

that   used without a comma to introduce a defining clause

which   preceded by a comma, used to introduce a descriptive clause

In his classic, *Modern English Usage,* Fowler takes *seven* pages to explain this; quite a few manuals shed similar amounts of ink over it. So you can read about it in tremendous detail elsewhere if you wish. The issue is whether one says "the book *that* I gave you" or "the book *which* I gave you." The short answer is that if you precede the word with a comma, it should be *which*. Otherwise you should use *that*. For example:

> *Beating the Street, which* I gave you for your birthday, is Peter Lynch's second book.

> The book *that* I gave you last week is out of print.

The long answer: *which* introduces a descriptive clause. Such a clause adds information that may be helpful but that could be omitted. *That* introduces restrictive, crucial information that cannot be omitted from the sentence. The first sentence, above, can stand alone without the *which* clause: the information in the clause is interesting and important but not necessary to the integrity of the sentence. We indicate that by using a comma or pair of commas. Without the *that* clause, the second sentence is meaningless. *What* book is out of print? The *that* clause is crucial to identifying the book. We emphasize the essential nature of such a clause by omitting a comma and using *that*.

A smart friend of mine notes that in business writing, *that* is probably the word we should be using most of the time. Her point is that we don't need any "by-the-way" additions. Information-intensive writing deals with crucial facts we can't omit. Her assertion puts her in good company: experts estimate that nine times out of ten, *that* will be correct. So try *that* first, and if it works, keep it.

■ **Abused.** Another way of putting it is **overused.** This category includes words that have been put together according to standard English principles, with results that have become faddish. In each case, the word given stands for a raft of similar ones.

impact, to The new edition of H.W. Fowler's classic, *Modern English Usage*, was taken to task by some critics when it appeared to be approving this use of *impact*. Note, however, that a cartoon in the *Wall Street Journal* considerably longer ago showed a manager telling his subordinate, "As I mentioned before, Fassler, you'll never go anywhere until you start using 'impact' as a verb." Take your choice. I'd be careful not to overexpose this and other noun-to-verb constructions. *Affect* is, by the way, a fine synonym for *impact*.

English is enormously flexible. One facet of its flexibility is the ability to take one part of speech and turn it into another, thus effectively creating a new word. Many words so created have become respectable residents of the dictionary. The practice adds to the texture and charm of English. I would advise, however, not overdoing the creativity thing by recklessly turning words into verbs, or as Calvin of the much-missed comic strip "Calvin and Hobbes" puts it, "verbing." As Calvin notes, "Verbing weirds language." How true, as the next example demonstrates.

incentivize Good grief. We have a perfectly nice word for this concept: *motivate*. Why do we need *incentivize*, which is hideously ugly? The original word was a noun, *incentive*, that got verbed—an egregious example of "izification," illustrating another strength of our language that all too easily becomes a liability.

Again in accordance with the rich traditions of English, which borrows liberally from every language it meets, our mother tongue happily incorporated the Romans' practice of adding suffixes to form new words. The result is such shockers as *incentivize*. As if prioritize and demilitarize weren't enough. Because these and many other "-izes" are included in good standing in most dictionaries, I can't forbid you to use them. But I do cordially counsel restraint. Limit yourself to one or two per communication, and for goodness' sake, don't start making up your own. There is no rational excuse for *Fidelityize* or *videoize*.

enthuse   More verbing. This back formation from *enthusiasm* pains a majority of the *American Heritage*'s Usage Panel. I'd avoid it.

intuit   Still more verbing. This one's been around for a long time, but the Usage Panel nonetheless dislikes it—and they're not alone. Another one to avoid.

-wise,   as in public education-wise. An infelicitous use of a principle similar to that which generates the *-izes*, above, though *-wise* typically creates temporary words—usually not great ones. My clever friend Connie, a writer, and other authorities on style feel that it should be avoided at all costs. I suggest avoiding it too whenever possible. At least don't use it if you can come up with something better. For example, which sentence is more appealing?

Consumers have become more careful *dollar-wise*.

Consumers are spending more carefully.

By comparison with the second sentence, the first seems lazy and imprecise. Perfectly all right for a first draft, but not for final copy.

▦ **Not to be used.** This category includes words that are not in the dictionary or are listed in it as "nonstandard." To me that's kiss-of-death time. Some are jargon, some are colloquial or dialect, some are simply errors. Unless you are certain you're writing to readers who share and appreciate your vocabulary, don't lead the dictionary. Eventually, if a word is derivatively sound and useful, it will find its way to a respectable listing in *American Heritage* or *Webster's*. Until then, don't use it. The list includes, but is by no means limited to, the following:

> alot
> alright
> anyways
> heighth
> incent
> irregardless
> nother, as in "a whole *nother*"
> regards, used in "in *regards* to"

▧ THE BOTTOM LINE ▧

▦ **Don't confuse, misuse, or abuse words.**

▦ **Don't use words that are substandard or nonexistent.**

▦ **Use this guide and your dictionary if you aren't sure.**

CHAPTER 6

Do I Have Too Many Words?

Too many words make for a fine first draft—easy and quick to write. A famous line, which I've heard attributed to everyone from Herodotus to Emerson to Ross Perot (what a crew!) is, "If I had had more time, I would have written you a shorter letter." Blaise Pascal said it first, or at least the gist of it. He wrote in 1657: "I've made this letter longer than usual, only because I didn't have time to make it shorter." Yes, it's tedious, time-consuming work to make something long shorter. To a great extent that's how I make my living, and that's why I get paid for it.

This doesn't mean you should try to limit your verbiage in your initial draft. Cut loose with that first fine careless rapture; get it down on paper, however windy you are with the words. Then get rid of the extra ones. That, of course, is where the art lies. You could say of good writing what Michelangelo said about sculpting: you just remove everything that isn't part of the statue. He also called sculpting "an art that takes away superfluous materials." That's exactly what you want to do.

Sounds easy. You know it isn't, either in constructing a great sculpture or creating a good piece of writing. Here are some strategies for chiseling away nonessential sentence elements.

▪ **Eliminate roundabout phrases.** The media constantly set us a bad example by using such phrases as "shower activity" and "accident scene." Even if they can't bring themselves to say that it's raining or somebody smashed up a car, why do they have to add the words "activity" and "scene"? Take these words out: do you miss them? Resist such phrases when you write: the media's bad behavior is no excuse for yours.

You add nothing but mass to your piece with the following phrases. They are rarely justified: note how easily you can edit them out—in itself a clue:

the field of	the sum of
the study of	it is
the fact is that	there is, there are

The field of science is a fascinating one.
Science is fascinating.

It is easy to see *that* the production department is understaffed.
The production department is clearly understaffed.

The fact is that it is as difficult as *it is* important
    to keep tight control of receivables.
Keeping tight control of receivables is important
    but difficult.

There are four keys *that* control movement for
this program.

Four keys control movement for this program.

Here are a few others and their space-saving equivalents:

it would be appreciated if	please
would you be so kind as to	please
in the approximate area of	about
in the majority of instances	usually
in the not-too-distant future	soon
at this point in time	at this time, now

Watch for these and similar phrases. Why add stuff without substance?

■ **Don't pile on pairs of negatives**. Writing with double negatives—"not unusual" for "usual"—is a stylistic tic dating back at least to the 18th century, when the phenomenon was discovered by Bishop Robert Loth. (I didn't make it up. Grammar people live for that kind of thing.) Anyway, double negatives verge on cute, and they take up room. They're out of place in business writing unless you're conveying a particularly fine shade of meaning. Often the meaning of a sentence is unchanged when you strike out pairs of negatives such as these:

We should *avoid prohibiting* people who are *not uncommitted* to the project from attending.

We should let people who are committed to the project attend.

Bruce was *not unfair* to his employees, and they expressed their *not insincere* appreciation.

Bruce was fair to his employees, and they expressed their sincere appreciation.

■ **Edit out "prepositional phrase freight."** In business writing, we're usually trying to give information. As a result, we're often tempted to try to convey just one more fact or suggestion, jam one more bit of helpful data, into a sentence. The writing becomes heavy and overloaded. Remember the five W's of journalism, who, what, where, when, and why? As I recall, you're supposed to incorporate all five into a lead mega-sentence for your article or press release. Unfortunately, it rarely works. Fitting that much information into one sentence typically results in an overweight construction:

> The leaders of the nations of the Pacific Rim will meet at a conference in a suburb of Seoul on June 19, 1999, to seek ways to cut the cost of durable goods that are intended for distribution to countries in the Western Hemisphere.

What we have here is a series of prepositional phrases strung together. You can recognize them by their form, which is very consistent: a small word, often one of location—*at, by, up, over, under, for, with*—and its object. The prepositional phrases in the sentence above are

of the nations	on June 19, 1999
of the Pacific Rim	of durable goods
at a conference	for distribution
in a suburb	to countries
of Seoul	in the Western Hemisphere

You can see that most of the sentence is prepositional phrase freight, and its weight has deep-sixed the sentence. You can do a lot to shrink or eliminate these phrases. Perhaps most easily, you can turn them into adjectives: the phrase "of the Pacific Rim" can become "Pacific Rim," "of Seoul" can become "Seoul"—or verbs: meet "at a conference" can be transformed into "confer."

Another smart move is to divide the data between two sentences.

> Leaders of the Pacific Rim nations will confer
> June 19, 1999, in a Seoul suburb. They will seek
> ways to cut the cost of durable goods distributed
> to countries in the Western Hemisphere.

Be wary, however, of going too far along this route. Draconian editing—ripping and chopping—is an activity to avoid. If you shrink and squeeze those prepositional phrases too far, your prose can eventually become all but impenetrable. The result is something that newsman Jack Hart engagingly refers to as "densepack" and I call the Black Hole School of Writing:

> Pacific Rim nation leaders confer in a Seoul sub-
> urb June 19, 1999, on cost-cutting measures tar-
> geted at Western Hemisphere durable goods
> distribution.

And what we have *here* is a failure to communicate. The new sentence is a sort of shorthand for the original, with something definitely lost in translation. In fact, it's practically impossible to translate. You can edit more gently and still keep to a reasonable length. With a reasonable hope of being understood.

Note that prepositional phrases don't always indicate a load of information. They may simply be the sign of a first draft, loosely put together and in need of tightening up on your next pass:

Loose: On Monday, September 2, the CEO of this company will give a presentation with slides to those of us in the areas of marketing and sales.

Edited: Our company CEO will give a slide presentation Monday, September 2, to our marketing and sales areas.

■ **Keep the action in your verbs.** Look at the following verb forms. They're wordy, and they're ineffective—an ugly combination:

> to have a tendency
> to be a participant
> to do an analysis
> to show a preference
> to give a demonstration

What's gone wrong? I'll tell you what. The verbs that should be the driving force or propulsion of the sentence have gone into hiding and reemerged as *nouns: preference, analysis.* Note that's where the action, such as it is, exists, not in the weak, action-poor verbs *to have, to be,* and so forth. As a result, the phrases are not only wordy, they are static, stripped of vigor. Here are the "real" verbs, restored to their proper places:

> to tend
> to participate
> to analyze
> to prefer
> to demonstrate

Shorter, stronger, and more interesting. Too many little helping verbs, such as *to do* or *to be,* can alert you to this flaw in your own writing.

Edit for all these indiscretions before you print your final draft. Be remorseless: not even you, let alone anyone else, will miss this stuff when it's gone.

THE BOTTOM LINE

- **Get rid of roundabout constructions.**
- **Eliminate double negatives.**
- **Unload prepositional phrase freight.**
- **Check that the action is in verbs, not nouns.**

CHAPTER 7

Have I Spiced My Writing with Variety?

If your boss complains that your writing lacks zip, or sex appeal, or pizzazz, it may be suffering a surfeit of sameness. In that case, you need to add some variety. Moderation's a key principle here—because if you use any technique *im*moderately, you're losing variety, not gaining it. Here are a few tips to inject the right level of this important commodity into your writing:

■ Vary your paragraphs in length. Everyone knows a certain amount of white space is a good thing for eye appeal and relief. Some people think you need to bullet out everything to achieve this. At the moment, I think, bulleting suffers from overexposure, and it adds to overall copy length. But the idea is basically a good one.

In fact, you can easily get white space by changing the configuration of your paragraphs. If you have a heavy block of text in which you have discussed three concepts, for instance, break it into three paragraphs, each with a topic sentence. While you're at it, use the topic sentence that applied to all three concepts as a one-sentence paragraph: very catchy. Visually, you'll get a design scheme that looks something like this:

XXXXX XXXXXX XXXXXXX XXXXXXXXX.

XXX XXXXXX XXXX XXX XXXXXXX XXXXXX
XXXX XXXXXXXX XX, XXX XXXX XXXXXXXXXXX
XXXXXXXX XX XXX XXXXX XX XXXXX.

XXXXXXXXX, XXXXXX XXX XXXXX XXXXXXX
XX XXX XXXXXXX XX XXXXXXXX XXXXXXXX
XXXX XXXX; XXXX XX XXXXXXXXXXX XX
XXXXX XXXXXXXX.

XXXX XX XXX XXXX XX XXXX XXXXXXXXXX XX
XXX XXXXXXX XXXX. XX XXX XXXXX XXXX XXX
XXXXXXX XXX XXXXX XXX XXXX.

instead of this:

XXXXX XXXXXX XXXXXXX XXXXXXXXX.
XXX XXXXXX XXXX XXX XXXXXXX XXXXXX
XXXX XXXXXXXX XX, XXX XXXX XXXXXXXXXXX
XXXXXXXX XX XXX XXXXX XX XXXXX.
XXXXXXXXX, XXXXXX XXX XXXXX XXXXXXX
XX XXX XXXXXXX XX XXXXXXXX XXXXXXXX
XXXX XXXX; XXXX XX XXX. XXXX XX XXX
XXXX XX XXXX XXXXXXXXXX XX XXX XXXXXXX
XXXX. XX XXX XXXXX XXXX XXX XXXXXXXXXX
XX XXXXXXX XXX XXXXX XXX XX XXXXX XXXXXXXX.

Depending on your needs for the piece as a whole, this could represent a welcome change. It's also useful if you're dealing with hard or unfamiliar concepts.

■ **Vary the length of your sentences.** Throw a short sentence in among the longer ones when you think of it. Business writing is almost by definition expository and information intensive: a short sentence gives readers a break. Also, particularly if you are dealing with material that's technical, or unfamiliar to your readers, be sure to shorten up sentences overall. A larger number of shorter sentences will be a blessing to them.

> The recent legislation, passed by an overwhelming majority in both houses and signed into law by the President in June, clarifies the tax status of certain types of insurance, allowing tax-favorable treatment similar to that already enjoyed by other forms of health insurance, and as such validates these types of coverage as mainstream insurance products.

Not a thing wrong with the grammar, but a reader who attempts it in one bite may require the Heimlich maneuver. Cut it into small pieces as an aid to digestion.

■ **Vary sentences in form.** It's unlikely to the vanishing point that readers will notice you're doing this. However, if you don't, your writing may bore them. A string of declarative sentences—I did this. He did that. The system crashed.—gets old. So does the overuse of any form, for that matter:

> *Barring an unforeseen change* in the money markets, our IPO should be quite successful. *Taking advantage of a lull* in the commodities market, we consider our timing to be unusually opportune. *Remembering our difficulties* in the past, we feel extremely fortunate.

And hoping to hear from you soon, we remain your humble servant. Stylistic tics such as this can actually be pretty annoying. You've got a whole range of ways to assemble thoughts into sentences that look and sound different. Here's a thought from an annual report, expressed in various ways:

> Our residential real estate loan business increased by $200 million as a result of mortgage refinancing.

> Bolstered by mortgage refinancing, our residential real estate loan business increased by $200 million.

> Our residential real estate loan business increased by $200 million. We attribute the rise to mortgage refinancing.

> We refinanced many mortgages, and our residential real estate loan business increased by $200 million.

■ **Vary word length.** The same principle applies to words. If they aren't varied in length, you are probably in trouble. Too many short words not only look bad, but may be a sign that you have not moved far enough from a loose, first-draft style. For instance, look at the following string of pearls:

> It is a bit of a reach to be in favor of the rights of the embezzler.

The series of short words looks choppy, feels wordy. On the flip side, look at the Cuisinart effect you get when you overdo long words:

> Hypervigilance ascertaining commodity availabil-
> ity effectually contravenes competitive challenges.

Chains of long words create a barrier: I think that ver-
bal logjam means something like keep an eye on supply
to stay even with the competition, but who has time to
translate?

One of my students complained, understandably,
"You won't let us use long words; now you won't let us
use short words. What words do you want me to use?" Of
course, I want you to use all of your words. In rotation. A
mix of long, short, and in-between words is easy on the
eye as well as the brain. A series of words all the same
length is a signal to rewrite.

■ **A note of caution: Don't think variety means everything but the kitchen sink.** Throwing every kind of font,
point size, and attention-getting format such as caps and
boldface type into your work in the name of variety is not
a good idea. Because word processing makes this instan-
taneous, the appeal can be seductive. From the reader's
standpoint, however, it's surprisingly distracting. Or let's
just say less is more. Here's what I mean:

> Get a comprehensive COMBINATION of finan-
> cial services with the **Bank of Virginia Premium
> Account**. This account lets you <u>combine *deposit*
> and *investmen*t balances to waive account fees.</u>

Goodness! the level of excitement is well-nigh intol-
erable. There's something endearingly Victorian about all
the body English, so to speak, but you can see that the
technique emphasizes form over substance. It also looks

as if the writer didn't trust the copy to speak for itself. Observe, shudder, abstain.

There you have the do's and don't's of variety. Check your writing to be sure you haven't hypnotized your readers with sameness or gone font-happy to attract their attention.

THE BOTTOM LINE

- Vary paragraph length, sentence length, sentence form, and word length.
- Don't overdo variety in font and type.

CHAPTER 8

When All's Said and Done, Have I Avoided Clichés to The Nth Degree?

Clichés are another dark side of variety that I didn't touch on in the last chapter because I wanted to give them their own—how shall I put it? place in the sun. (As you see, I write all my own stuff.) Clichés are phrases that once were sharp, meaningful, clever. Over time they have lost their luster. Worse, they have almost lost their meaning. Let me elaborate. Take the cliché "My heart skipped a beat," for example. When people first began using it, the metaphor referred to an experience that is truly dramatic. If it's ever happened to you, you know what I mean. Your body shudders at the impact of the arrhythmia produced under the stress of a powerful, emotional moment. Originally the phrase was used to authenticate the intensity of such a moment—the moment when a child stepped out in front of a moving vehicle or a message arrived saying All is lost, or All is OK. People who had felt heart arrhythmia could relate to this; people who hadn't were awed as well. Alas for the effectiveness of the phrase today—it's been so overused and has lost so much altitude that it now has almost no emotive impact. Someone is likely to say, "My heart skipped a beat when I thought I might miss lunch."

Variety is the spice of life. All the world's a stage. Through a glass darkly. It's as plain as the nose on your face. To be or not to be? She's the cream of the crop. When they were new, these phrases engaged the senses and heart. The first person who told someone else to have a nice day probably got credit for thoughtfulness approaching sainthood. Nowadays people say they've made other plans. The other day I saw a bus I hoped to take. Straining to see the destination in the display slot above the windshield, I read "Have a Nice Day." Not very helpful. In fact, terminally annoying. (I think that's a pun. I get credit, even though it was accidental.)

But what are you going to do? How are you, have a nice day, please don't hesitate to call, all are coins of the realm—you should pardon the expression—in conversation and writing. They move the action along smoothly, if not interestingly. This is a point I appreciate. I'm requesting just three things:

■ **Keep the numbers down.** Don't string clichés together. You can create a series of them like lily pads on a pond, and leapfrog from one to another without ever coming up with one original thought:

Last but not least, please rest assured that our group stands ready to do everything in our power to ensure that a good time is had by all.

Finally, we'd like to assure you our group will do everything we can to ensure a wonderful evening for the Emerald Shillelagh reunion.

■ **Be sure the cliché is appropriate.** Sentences such as the following are unsuitable in a business context:

My better half and I look forward to filling the cup with you and your bride on Saturday.

You asked why our sales went through the roof in May. That's the $64,000 question, without a doubt—but it sure beats the heck out of me, chief.

Save the arch and the poetic, the catch phrase and the referential dialogue for your friends, if you must. (Actually, if you write like this, you may not have any. A lot of people don't appreciate this stuff from their friends either.)

My wife and I look forward to dinner with you and Mrs. Archer on Saturday.

You asked why sales increased in May. It's an excellent question, to which I have no answer.

■ **Reword clichés when you can.** Your writing will be fresher and more memorable. As you can see from the fixes above, it's not even hard. It just means you have to go off autopilot and think about what you're saying. Now that your consciousness has been raised, it should be easy to recognize *welcome aboard, look before we leap, put a game plan in place,* etc., for the tired, stale material it is. You can do better, and you should.

▨ THE BOTTOM LINE ▨

- ▪ **Watch the clichés you use: keep the numbers down.**
- ▪ **Be sure a cliché is business-appropriate.**
- ▪ **Reword clichés if possible.**

CHAPTER 9

Have I Created Unintentional "Noise"?

This chapter is short, but that doesn't mean it's not important. Especially if you're in a hurry or just writing carelessly, you can produce unintentional sound effects, which I call noise. Such tunes and rhythms are unwanted additions to your writing because they distract readers from your points. Needless to say, you can also come across as less than serious or committed in your intent. The charms of frivolity are pretty much lost on captains of industry (see "If you must be funny," in Chapter 3). Your boss is probably no exception, so watch out for noise.

Noise can be easily edited out by reading copy aloud. You can also read it to yourself—I read all my own writing and everyone else's "aloud to myself"—because actually you're editing for noise your readers may hear when reading to *them*selves. (I'm assuming they won't be reading your work aloud, but that could happen as well—maybe in a meeting, where you'd be horribly embarrassed if you'd written in iambic pentameter and hadn't meant to. If you meant to, you have a career problem, or you will soon [see "captains of industry" above]). Here are three areas to monitor:

■ **Achieving accidental alliteration.** I was kidding. But that's a fair example. Alliteration, a string of words with the same first letter, creates terrific poetry and tongue twisters—two things you absolutely don't want in your writing:

> Sarah will sit in on the secretaries' session of the
> seminar Saturday.

Read the words to yourself and you'll see the unpleasant effect of the repeated sibilant *s:* a delivery annoying enough to obscure the message. Edit for the repetition. (No fair changing Sarah's name or the day of the session.) Here's a great use for your Thesaurus command, by the way. If they don't immediately spring to mind, you can look up synonyms for at least every other offending word. Here's one tolerable rewrite:

> Sarah plans to attend the secretaries' portion of
> the conference on Saturday.

The fix isn't hard. Just be on the lookout for the problem.

■ **Overworking a vowel sound.**

> This conference offers an optimum opportunity to
> cost out promising software.

The proliferation of short *o* sounds is liable to take a reader's mind off the content of your sentence. Rewrite:

> You'll have an excellent chance to price attractive
> software at this conference.

▓ **Breaking into rhythm or rhyme.** As I mentioned, business writers shouldn't write poetry. You want to be known for your lean, terse prose. That means editing to control this sort of thing:

> We see all three in the '93 fee.

> Sell Morrell and O'Dell will rebel.

> Our income is well diversified, small banking business aside.

Let's see. We could change to

> All three of these changes are reflected in the fee schedule for 1993.

> If we put the Morrell division up for sale, we'll get resistance from O'Dell.

and

> Apart from our small banking business, our income is well diversified.

As always, the problem is easy to see and hear in someone else's work, so read your own as if you were an outsider. Remind yourself of the issue as you revise, and *listen* to what you've written.

❀ THE BOTTOM LINE ❀

▓ **Avoid beginning several words in a sentence with the same letter.**
▓ **Rewrite to edit out an oversupply of one vowel sound.**
▓ **Guard against creating accidental rhythms or rhymes.**

CHAPTER 10

Have I Venerated the Sacred Cows of Writing?

G. K. Chesterton said, "There are three rules of good writing, and nobody knows what they are." There are, however, a few rules that everybody seems to know. Interestingly enough, these rules haven't always been historically observed, nor is there general agreement that they are justified. In some cases, there's not even a legitimate grammatical or logical reason for them. Nevertheless, if enough people are convinced of something, for all practical purposes it becomes a rule.

Because I believe in writing defensively and not stirring anybody up if I don't have to, I try to observe these rules—as long as it doesn't cause me pain or do violence to my sentence structure. I strongly suggest you do the same in the following areas. Why lay yourself open to criticism, justified or not? The cows follow.

■ **Don't split infinitives.** The infinitive form of a verb is *to* and whatever: to wait, to invite, to promote. Since in Latin this form is expressed in one word, some 19th-century grammarians decided that these two parts of English verbs should not be split by an adverb, such as *really:* to *really* know. Since English is not Latin, nor even a Romance language, I don't think that's much of a justification for the rule. It does, however, make sense in certain cases where the two verb halves are widely split and a misreading is possible. For example:

> She has agreed *to* with much enthusiasm in the future *search* for a new account manager.

You can see that *to search* gets lost as a verb because the split is so wide, and it's possible to read *future search* incorrectly as a noun. An infinitive split such as *to quickly move,* or *to simply ask,* on the other hand, seems relatively harmless.

Authors of style manuals unanimously agree there are many things worse than a split infinitive, including stilted and obvious efforts to avoid one, but for some reason people remember the no-splitting rule from grade school. I knew a CEO who got a sharply critical letter from the same customer every time his huge retail organization split an infinitive in promotional copy—ads, letters, etc.—as if the CEO were personally responsible for each of the splits. Since the CEO happened to know a lot about language and writing, but couldn't keep an eye on all company copy writers, this annoyed him. Clearly, people not only remember the rule, they *like* remembering it and enjoy criticizing people who fail to observe it. Since I can't afford to have people criticizing my grammar, I always rephrase to avoid a split. Since you can't afford it either, go ahead and rewrite to reconnect or eliminate a split infinitive. It's almost always easy.

> I'd like you *to generally brief* the consultant on our progress to date.

Here you can probably omit the splitter, *generally,* which adds little substance anyhow.

> Was it wise *to conveniently "forget"* his prison record?

A more interesting problem. *Conveniently* fits naturally where it is, not very comfortably elsewhere: I'm sure that's where one would place it in a conversation.

Yet to avoid the appearance of incorrect writing, I'd rewrite. There are plenty of ways to do this:

> I question the wisdom of conveniently "forgetting" his prison record.

> Was it wise to "forget" his prison record so conveniently?

> You've conveniently "forgotten" his prison record. Is that wise?

■ **Never end a sentence with a preposition.** This means concluding with one of those little words, often words of location: *over, under, around, in.* "Preposition overhang" slides by easily in conversation, and it feels natural: "This company has nothing to be ashamed of"; "I've forgotten what I came for." When you write, you may have a problem, because your boss, or your reader, may perceive it as incorrect. Here are two more examples of preposition overhang:

I can't decide which slide to end *with*.

The senior account executive justifiably resents having been lied *to*.

Historical precedents abound for ending sentences with prepositions. Shakespeare did it in Hamlet's soliloquy, citing "The heartache and the thousand natural shocks/That flesh is heir to. . . ." Our forefathers did it. Here's Benjamin Franklin: "Do not squander time, for that's the stuff life is made of." Churchill is said to have famously growled that the supposed rule was "the sort of English up with which I will not put," illustrating the potentially stilted results of observing it. As for current examples, that pundit of the proper, *National Review* editor William F. Buckley, Jr., says in his recent book, *The Right Word*, "It is not a sign of arrogance for the king to rule. That is what he is there for." And English playwright Alan Bennett writes in *Writing Home,* "One of the exercises in rehearsal required each member of the cast to . . . shout out at the top of his voice the worst thing he could think of."

To all these distinguished people, ending with a preposition is no sin at all. In the 1700s, however, John Dryden, "probably on the basis of a specious analogy to Latin," notes the *American Heritage Dictionary* (those Romans again), invented the rule against ending with a preposition. Heady times for sure, when the poet laureate gets to go around making up grammar rules. I missed my century. I will concede that you can get some unlovely sentences ending in prepositions, which is probably why Dryden thought up his rule. Here's another famous example. The young child says to the parent:

> What did you bring that book I didn't want to be
> read *to out of up for?*

Five prepositions in a row, and the effect is predictably ugly. But more to the point, plenty of people learned that ending with a preposition is not just awkward, it's *wrong*. So, if you can comfortably rewrite so as to avoid flouting this rule, even though it's based on a "specious premise," why not?

> I can't decide which slide to use in conclusion.

> The senior account executive justifiably resents
> the lies she was told.

Use your ingenuity to block potential criticism of preposition overhang.

■ **Don't begin a sentence with a conjunction, such as** *and* **or** *but.* Again, it's the amorphous "they" who say you mustn't do it. We can only speculate about where this one got going. The authors of the Bible, the framers of the Constitution and the Bill of Rights, and Abraham Lincoln were all apparently unaware of this injunction and began sentences with *and, or , so, for,* etc., with impunity. And if they weren't divinely inspired, who is?

> And God said, Let there be light: and there was
> light.
> —Genesis 1:1

But in a larger sense, we cannot consecrate, we
cannot hallow. . . .

—Abraham Lincoln, the Gettysburg Address

Most reputable grammarians call the rule nonsense,
and I have trouble with it, too: it seems particularly capricious and ill-founded. In fact, you can find sentences
beginning with *and, or,* and *but* throughout this book: but
that's primarily because I knew I'd have a chance to
explain on this page. I'd advise you, particularly if you're
trying hard to please, to edit out starting conjunctions—
unless you're quite confident your reader (or your boss)
is not a grammar amateur, or you're writing very infor-
mally. Starting with conjunctions flies well, for example,
in ad copy:

> We'll give you the first six issues free! *But* that's
> not all! You'll also receive our quarterly newslet-
> ter—a $20 value—at no charge.

■ **Avoid beginning a sentence with *however.*** Who
thought up this loser? "They" again. But since a number
of people are convinced it's correct, get along by going
along. It's perfectly simple to move the word from the
head of the sentence to some more innocuous place:

> *However,* I feel that the technical superiority of
> the product more than offsets the higher cost.

> I feel, *however,* that the . . .

Obviously, where all these sacred cows are concerned,
I belong to the Neville Chamberlain school of grammar:
peace at any price.

◸ THE BOTTOM LINE ◹

Why risk offending picky readers? Write out

- ■ split infinitives
- ■ sentences that end with *for, of,* or some other preposition
- ■ sentences that start with *and, but,* or some other conjunction
- ■ sentences that start with *however*

CHAPTER 11

Have I Dealt Carefully with Pronouns?

Pronoun problems are a grammar issue, which means there are clear rules about right and wrong, and pronouns can be tricky. They are virtually all we have left of English as the inflected language it once was: English word endings used to change, like those of Latin, depending on how the word was used in a sentence. Today's English mercifully doesn't do that, except for these small, important words. That's why we have three forms for most pronouns: *he* for the subject, or doer of the action, *him* for the object, the receiver of the action (including objects of prepositions), and *his* for the possessive, the owner of whatever. Here they are, for the record:

	SUBJECT	OBJECT	POSSESSIVE
Singular	I	me	mine
	you	you	yours
	he, she, it	him, her, it	his, hers, its
	who	whom	whose
Plural	we	us	ours
	you	you	yours
	they	them	theirs
	who	whom	whose

The words in column 2 substitute for the initiator of action: "John/*He* hit the wall." Those in column 3 are for the receiver of action: "The nature of the error hit Sarah/*her*." Those in column 4 express possession: "The book is John and Sarah's/The book is *theirs*."

In a conversation, you can usually get away with making pronoun errors—unless, of course, you are speaking with a fastidious person who hates "Between you and I." If you are writing, however, you document an error clearly and more or less permanently.

To escape this fate, here are my suggestions for cleansing your work of the most irritating and incorrect pronoun mistakes.

■ **Note that the possessive pronouns take NO apostrophes.** We normally make possessive forms by adding an apostrophe or an apostrophe and *s*. Not to pronouns. Never, never. As I mentioned, they're old forms, and they're irregular. You will never be called upon to write *your's*, *her's*, *it's* (in the sense of *belonging to it*), or *their's*. You can comfortably assume that for all practical purposes these words simply *don't exist*. (In certain cases, a linguist might need them, but I can't conceive of any use for them in business writing.)

■ **Scrutinize pronoun pairs for case agreement.** How often have you heard, from the mouths of babes, as it were, "Her and me want to go to the mall"? I hope not very. Interestingly, surely not even the worst offenders would say, "*Her* wants to go" or "*Me* want to go." The trouble occurs when a pronoun is *paired* with another pronoun, or a noun, as in "*Janet and me* want to go." So the fix is easy: simply make sure each pronoun is correct alone. If you have written

> The lawyer requested postponement of the court date for *John and I,*

separate *I* from *John*. Now try reading the sentence:

> . . . postponement of the court date for *I.*

Oops. If it doesn't work without *John*, it's incorrect with him. "John and *me*" is correct. Here's another:

> *He and she* started work in this office in September 1989.

Divide and conquer: "*He* started," "*She* started." That sentence is fine as written.

It's the same for such constructions as "*Us Tareyton smokers* would rather fight than switch," an ad that upset a few grammarians, amateur and professional. Again, just separate the two elements, *Us* and *Tareyton smokers.* "*Us* would rather fight"? Me don't think so. "*We* Tareyton smokers." Here's another example:

> The accountant asked *we consultants* about our expense reports.

Split 'em up: "The accountant asked *we* . . ." Not good. "*Us* consultants" is correct. With this exercise of unpairing, you can solve The Case of the Paired Pronoun every time.

■ **Make sure your pronouns agree in number with the subject they represent:** A pronoun is a stand-in for someone or something previously mentioned:

Julia is a Chartered Financial Analyst. *She* got her degree at Brandeis.

Simply put, we don't say "Julia . . . he" or "Julia . . . they." Clear enough. Problems arise at least in part, I suspect, as a result of the feminists' refusal to accept the time-honored *he* as a generic reference to a person of unknown gender. This makes people want to say, "When the new manager comes aboard, *they*," which may be politically correct but is grammatically unconscionable. See Chapter 14 for some easy and grammatical fixes that will pass the scrutiny of the PC police.

■ **Department of Details. Watch out for three frequently misused pronouns:**

1. **myself:** Two good uses for this pronoun include emphasis:

   I *myself* was unable to make the trip, but our senior vice president went.

   and reflexivity, or doing something to oneself:

   I asked *myself* why I had established *myself* in this backwater town.

   Bad uses include using *myself* as a substitute for *I* or *me*:

   Steve and *myself* will stop by your desk once you're settled.

   She wanted Mike and *myself* to provide detail on the systems conversion.

Using *myself* this way, as the *American Heritage Dictionary*'s Usage Panel comments, "can indicate pomposity or a sense of importance." Do you want people to think you're that kind of person? Not I myself! (Besides, I admire the Usage Panel extravagantly—it includes William Safire, Daniel Patrick Moynihan, Jeanne Kirkpatrick, Eudora Welty, William Zinsser, and 50 other smart, literate people—so its collective opinion rates high with me.)

2. **who** and **whom**: Calvin Trillin says the word *whom* was invented to make everyone sound like a butler. In other words, snootier than thou. That's pretty funny, and I'll concede he has a point. But we still need *whom* as well as *who* in our writing. Our language is not so debased that we can't remember, at least in writing, to distinguish between the subject and the object pronoun. Write *who* if you'd write *she*. Write *whom* if you'd write *her*. It's simple enough, though you may have to do a little shuffling of word order. Let's try a couple of examples:

I interviewed the man *who/m* you recommended.

Substitute *she* you recommended, then invert the order: you recommended *she*—uh oh. That's clearly wrong. *Her* you recommended, you recommended *her*. Equally clearly, that's right. Therefore the word you should use is *whom*.

Try this one:

Who/m is the best technician on your team?

She is the best technician? Exactly. Use *who*.

An aside on the spoken word. Some people, apparently going Mr. Trillin one better, believe that *whom* has the upper-crust sound of an English butler and is therefore to be preferred on all occasions. (It's part of the American inferiority complex that makes us watch Mobil Masterpiece Theater compulsively and think everyone with an English accent is smarter than we are.) You will indeed sound like a butler, but an ungrammatical one, if you go around asking on the telephone, "*Whom* shall I say is calling?" Substitute another pair of pronouns: *She* is calling or *her* is calling? It's *who*. Incidentally, "May I tell him who is calling?" avoids the problem. I don't even like to ask who's calling: my mother told me it's rude, but we're dealing with the business world, not the genteel South where she learned manners.

3. **who-** and **whomever**: If you want to use these words—and I'm not saying you must if you don't want to—you should know there's a trick involved, case-wise. (My friend Connie, who objects to -*wise*—see Chapter 5—is far from alone. Connie-wise, I'm behaving badly.) Their usage depends, once again, on whether the word is functioning as a subject or an object pronoun. The pronoun *who-ever*, like *who*, stands for the subject, the initiator of the action. *Whomever* is, like *whom*, the object or recipient of action. Most of the time you can decide, as with *who* and *whom*, by substituting a

more familiar pair of pronouns, such as *he* and *him:*

Whoever wants it can have the Windsor account.

Because the type of pronoun that could substitute for *who(m)ever* is a subject pronoun—*he* wants, not *him* wants—the correct word is *whoever*, not *whomever*.

The children begged *whomever* they saw to take them swimming.

Substitute *he* or *him*: they saw *him*, therefore *whomever*.

But trouble comes with a sentence such as this:

Mrs. Tilledge shows *who(m)ever* visits the store her horrible-looking grandchildren's pictures.

Whoever is correct here, as it's the subject of the verb "visits" (*he* visits, *we* visit), but "shows *whoever*" rightly bothers people who are inclined to dwell on things. Shouldn't the word be the object of the verb "shows"? In which case, wouldn't "shows *whom*ever" be correct, just as you'd say "shows *me*" or "shows *him*"? An excellent question.

The key to this puzzle is that *whoever* is leading a bigamous double life. It is simultaneously both the object of what comes *before* it, Mrs. Tilledge's showing, and the subject of what comes *after*, the visiting. As some grammar books put it, the word "squints" in both directions. This can make it hard to determine at a glance whether you should use *whoever* or *whomever*.

Here is a simple way to get it right every time. Give yourself a "shadow" person to operate as the object of whatever may come before: say Harvey, Jimmy Stewart's imaginary rabbit. Or your sister, or The Artist Formerly Known as Prince. Who(m)ever. Then, when you're uncertain whether to use *whoever* or *whomever*, substitute "Harvey, *who*" or Harvey, *whom*." *Who*, remember, is the subject, the *I/he/they* pronoun case, *whom* the object, or *me/him/them* one.

You may not want to think too hard about this—just do it. It's 100 percent effective:

Mrs. Tilledge asks ___?___(Harvey, WHO) visits the store . . . asks *who*ever visits

The lobsters are ready for __?___(Harvey, WHO) wants one . . . for *who*ever wants.

I told ___?__(Harvey, WHOM) I saw about the wedding . . . *whom*ever I saw.

Did you ask ___?___(Harvey, WHO) is downstairs to come up . . . *who*ever is downstairs.

Remember, you never, ever have to use *who(m)ever* if it makes you unhappy. Mrs. Tilledge could just as easily show "everybody who visits," lobsters are ready "if you want one," and you can "ask the guests downstairs to come up." Edit the pesky pair out of your writing entirely, if you like. If you do use them, however, use them correctly.

Attention to these highlights in the secret life of pronouns should keep you more or less entirely out of trouble.

▨ THE BOTTOM LINE ▨

- Be aware that pronouns change form depending on their use in your sentence.
- Remember that possessive pronouns *(its, theirs, etc.)* take no apostrophes.
- Unpair nouns and pronouns to be sure your pronoun's in the right case.
- Make sure a pronoun agrees with its subject in number (not "everybody . . . they").
- If you use them, pay special attention to *myself, who(m)*, and *who(m)ever.*

CHAPTER 12

Am I Making Good or Bad Use of Repetition?

When there's a reason for it, repetition can be an effective aid to communication.

■ **Use repetition to reinforce a message.** As a rhetorical device, repetition can help make a message powerful and memorable. It's a time-honored tradition that dates from the Bible and the classics:

> Blessed are the poor in spirit, for theirs is the kingdom of heaven.
>
> Blessed are they that mourn, for they shall be comforted.
>
> Blessed are the meek, for they shall inherit the earth.
> —Matthew 5:1–3
>
> A horse, a horse! my kingdom for a horse!
> —*Richard III,* iv, 7

Repetition can reinforce a message with considerable strength. During the Battle of Britain in World War II, Winston Churchill made use of it in speeches that inspired and encouraged his countrymen in England's "darkest hour":

> We shall fight them on the beaches; we shall fight on the landing grounds, we shall fight in the fields and in the streets, we shall fight in the hills; we shall never surrender.

You can make repetition work for you in business writing, also, if less dramatically:

> We can improve our visibility by targeting proper market segments. We can improve our sales volume by increased efforts among Fortune 1000 companies. And we can improve delivery by making the best use of our distribution channels.

■ **Use repetition to contribute to clarity.** As I said in Chapter 7, variety isn't always a good thing. It makes a certain amount of sense to identify things—be they systems, new projects, products, whatever—using the same word, to assure that readers understand you. It's definitely better than selecting a synonym no one understands. I read some ad copy from a bank that referred to "checks," then to "demand deposit forms." I had no idea you could call a check that, and neither do most people. Your word of first choice may well be the best, anyway: there's a reason why you chose it first, after all. Especially if you're writing about something new or unfamiliar, using the same word to refer to it is a service to your readers.

> Remove the lock on the reverse side of the *keyboard*. Use the coiled cord to connect the *input device* to the 686SX terminal.

If I think about it, I can deduce that the input device must be the keyboard—but I don't want to *have* to think about it. I'd rather the instructions read *keyboard* in both places.

Do not under any circumstances be deceived into thinking you must come up with a new synonym each time for literary reasons. Adherents to what I call the Chronologically Challenged Tiny Person School of Writing will tie themselves in knots inventing one synonym after another, increasingly preposterous, for an ordinary word such as "baby." Come on. You are not Shakespeare, and you are not writing *King Lear.* You're a business writer conveying information. The contrived synonyms aren't really any more euphonious anyway, in most cases; in fact, they're usually so obvious as to be distracting. If it's a baby, keep calling it a baby. There's nothing inelegant or illiterate about that kind of repetition.

On the other hand, don't risk alienating your audience by *needlessly* repeating an idea or word. Redundancy is bad repetition because it's obvious, pointless, and slipshod. For example, "You're invited to repeat your presentation again" is apt only if the presentation has been made twice already. *Innovative new idea* means *new new idea.* And I'm worn out from fighting the advertising folks who want to direct-mail *free gifts* to the public. If it isn't *free*, it isn't much of a gift. (Actually, given the Trojan horses most of these gifts turn out to be—a credit card free of annual fees [for now], a subscription with "no obligation," and so forth, all with unpleasant side effects—my point may be moot.) Here are some redundancies to avoid in your writing:

advance planning	join together
at this moment in time	must first be preceded
basically and funda-	mutual cooperation
mentally	other alternative
both . . . as well as	past history
consensus of opinion	repeat again
cooperate together	small in size
first and foremost	the reason why is
free of charge	because
future projections	two different kinds
general overview	usual custom
inadvertent error	X:00 A.M. in the
initially begin	morning
in X years from now	X:00 P.M. in the after-
innovative new	noon

Check carefully to be sure you've used repetition to reinforce and communicate, rather than simply to bloat your piece with unnecessary words.

▨ THE BOTTOM LINE ▨

▤ **Use repetition as a rhetorical device to reinforce your message.**

▤ **For clarity, repeat your word of choice instead of contriving synonyms.**

▤ **Don't repeat pointlessly: avoid redundant words and phrases.**

CHAPTER 13

Have I Used Parallel Construction for Correctness and Charm?

In the preceding chapter, we discussed repetition of words or phrases as an aid to communicating your message. Repetition of *form,* or parallel construction, can help deliver a strong message as well. Parallelism is the doctrine that says if you're using words or phrases in a sentence in the same way, they should be equivalent in form for appeal and effect. In other words, it's better to write

> John is helpful, hardworking, and reputable.

than

> John is helpful, a man who works hard, and of good reputation.

The three adjectives in the first example are parallel in form. In the second series, John *is* all three things. Yet because the first is an adjective, the second a noun form, and the third a prepositional phrase, the sentence, though grammatically correct, is awkward and lacking in style.

■ **Parallel elements make your message strong and appealing.** Parallel construction is a device used by speechmakers, often combined with apt word repetition, to deliver points with eloquence and style. Abraham Lincoln used it to magnificent effect. The Gettysburg Address, depending on how you count, contains at least 17 examples of parallelism, of which the most famous is probably "government of the people, by the people, and for the people." What if Lincoln had said "populist government, people-driven, and for the people"? I'm guessing it wouldn't have made *Bartlett's Familiar Quotations*.

■ **Nonparallel can mean ungrammatical.** In some cases, the lack of parallel form results in ungrammatical or illogical combinations. This error, sometimes called a *false series*, is often the result of haste or halfway editing. Such bad stuff as the following can result:

> The company has installed a new cafeteria, a fitness center, and a modular conference center is being planned.

The writer apparently planned to list several new areas *the company has installed,* began in style by listing two, then wandered off into a whole new clause. As a result, the sentence isn't coherent. You can't *install a new modular conference center is being planned,* yet that's the third "item" listed.

The bad apple in the bunch isn't always the last in a series:

> You can use the automated teller machine to get cash, deposits, and transfer funds.

Here the culprit is *deposits*. *Get cash* and *transfer funds* are matching items, verb forms following *to*. Alas, you can't *to deposits*.

In vertical listings, the problem sometimes worsens:

> This afternoon's meeting agenda includes
> - reading the minutes of the last meeting
> - begin budget allocation
> - business plan for upcoming fiscal year
> - we'll discuss vacation schedules

Only the first of the agenda items can actually be read with the sentence heading. That's careless, unattractive, and incorrect. We already know what your boss would have to say about this one.

■ **"Go vertical" to identify nonparallel sentence elements.** How can you identify faulty parallels in your own writing? It's easy to spot and fix the problem in a vertical list, so let's start with one of those. Here's an agenda from the general manager's office:

> Monday's meeting will feature
> - a report by the Buildings and Grounds Committee
> - a showing of our new recruitment video
> - three short presentations on new markets
> - Treasurer Freddie Folsom will provide a financial update

Our manager's assistant, who drafted this agenda, almost made it through Monday's agenda in style, but tripped over Freddie Folsom. Look at the heading, *Monday's meeting will feature.* Everything that follows that heading must complement it, or join logically with it. In other words, you must be able to read the header aloud coherently with *every single part* of the list that follows. The first three work fine: *Monday's meeting will feature a report by the Buildings and Grounds Committee* and so on. *Monday's meeting will feature Treasurer Freddie Folsom will provide a financial update,* however, is gibberish in my book and yours, too, if you're well rested and not too hassled. (That last condition's important: as I said, hasty writing is often at the root of faulty parallel structure.)

Let's move from a vertical list to a series. Editing out faulty parallels in a series isn't really difficult either: a similar principle applies. Take the sentence

> The new LAN administrator is efficient, experienced, and does her job well.

This sentence is actually a list in a horizontal form. Its heading, *The new LAN administrator is,* introduces a series of three items describing the new employee. According to the doctrine of parallelism, these three should be expressed in the same form. If you want to make the scheme perfectly clear, a good stratagem is actually to write the sentence in vertical list form. So let's "go vertical" with the sentence:

> The new LAN administrator is
>   efficient

> experienced [and]
> does her job well

The introductory phrase *The new LAN administrator is* obviously works with *efficient;* it works with *experienced*; but *The new LAN administrator is does her job well* doesn't make sense. On the other hand you can change that third phrase and say, *is efficient, experienced, and good at her job.* Now the introductory phrase makes sense with all three items.

Another way to fix faulty parallelism is to change the introductory phrase itself. Suppose we change the phrase in this case to read, *The new LAN administrator . . .* Change the second of the three parallel items so they read

> is efficient
> has experience [and]
> does her job well

To make sure we've got this issue pinned to the ground, let's try putting another of the sentences criticized above into vertical list form:

> You can use the automated teller machine to get
> cash, deposits, and transfer your funds.

We take it vertical to give ourselves the best visibility on the items involved:

> You can use the automated teller machine to get
>   cash
>   deposits
>   transfer your funds

Sorry, but you can't say that. You don't *to get deposits* or *to get transfer your funds.*

Try another introduction:

> You can use the automated teller machine to
>> get cash
>> deposits
>> transfer your funds

Now we have only one item that doesn't work: *deposits.* If we alter that to read *make deposits,* we have a hit on our hands:

> You can use the automated teller machine to
>> get cash
>> make deposits
>> transfer your funds

You can also change the introductory line and the last item so the sentence reads

> You can use the automated teller machine for
>> cash withdrawals
>> deposits
>> fund transfers

Now all you have to do is write out in horizontal form any of the lists that read correctly, choosing whichever you like best. You may not need to put your sentence into a vertical list form each time you're uncertain. But it is a handy way to see clearly what goes wrong in a nonparallel series. In any case, that's how it works.

Keep an eye on any series of two, three, or more items in your writing and raise your consciousness so you're able to recognize nonparallel structures when they pop up. Often this happens as the result of adding yet another piece of information to what's already written. When it does, your communication suffers. If you find nonparallel constructions in your work, use this mental geometry to straighten them out.

▦ THE BOTTOM LINE ▦

- Use parallel structure to give strength and appeal to your writing.
- Avoid the ungrammatical and/or illogical false series.
- Try listing items in a series vertically if you're not sure they're parallel.

CHAPTER 14

What's My OQ (Offense Quotient)?

Read this section carefully to avoid embarrassing your organization, your boss, and yourself. Read it also to avoid hurting other people's feelings.

I've touched elsewhere on the subject of not upsetting people, and I hope I've convinced you it's a good idea. In America today, unfortunately, not upsetting people is not easy. Lashed on by the proponents of political correctness, we've hit such a pitch of sensitivity that half our citizens are poised to be hurt and the other half are terrified of hurting them. It's so easy to offend someone along racial, ethnic, residential, gender, health, and sexual preference lines that it's a wonder anyone stumbles through a page of work clean. Press on regardless. And as you go, try not to make an issue of things one way or another. Be politically correct, in other words, but not so noticeably that you appear strident or in-your-face to those who are tired of politically correct. Take as your mantra the aspiration of Ezra Tull in Anne Tyler's *Dinner at the Homesick Restaurant*: "I'm trying to get through life as a liquid." Slip through as innocuously as you can.

I'll highlight a few spots where trouble can erupt and make some suggestions for slipping through. Let's begin with the issue of gender, since everybody has one and most people accordingly feel they have the right to an opinion.

■ **Gender: titles and pronouns.** It makes practical sense to be gender tender. I think the issue is less of a hot button than it has been, and a lot of people as old as I am never really cared in the first place. But you never know. So especially if you're writing to an unknown person or audience, it pays to try not to annoy in either direction. You don't know whether you've got a diehard feminist on your hands or a Marabel Morgan (the one who puts on babydoll pajamas and greets her mate at the door with a martini).

Take social titles: specifically, the Ms./Mrs./Miss by which you address female persons. Women sometimes call me in a snit—in snits, I suppose—because I've referred to them in an in-house newsletter I write for as "Ms." They are *Mrs.* Smith, they want me to know, and they hope I will be able to remember that henceforth, and so on in the same vein. Others call in snits, as you can probably guess, because I called them "Miss." Don't I realize that this outmoded label is offensive in the workplace? What business is anyone's marital status to anyone else? Do men have a title that shows whether *they* are married? And on. As I said, you never know.

By all means avoid using the pronouns *he, his,* and *him* when referring to an unspecified person or a category: "The customer service rep asks *his* callers. . . ." But you can err on the other side of this conundrum as well. The *Mrs.* Smith crowd, as you might expect, tend to view *him or her* with a jaundiced eye, as a kowtow to feminism. Even those who don't much care find it bulky and distracting, especially if it's repeated. I won't take sides on the issue, but such awkward and obvious constructions as *he/she* or *he and she,* especially when used repeatedly, really are distracting. The alternative, too often, is a default to the plural, generic *they/them/their,* yielding such incorrect and unlovely stuff as the following:

> When *a student* turns 19, *they* are no longer eligible for a free checking account.

> A new *staff member* often asks if *they* may be included in peer support training.

I appreciate the wish to be gender-sensitive that prompts these errors, but that doesn't make them any less wrong. The solution is to run around the issue by means of several helpful tricks. Try instead:

> **Plural:** When students turn 19, they are no longer . . .

> **Second person:** When you turn 19, you are no longer . . .

> **Rewrite:** A student who turns 19 is no longer . . .

▪ **Gender: occupations and positions.** Again, watch out for assumptions. Don't write as if you're surprised by *any*one's job: *woman doctor, woman lawyer* imply—a pretty outdated implication, by the way—that these professions are unusual for a woman. By the same token, *male nurse* and *male exotic dancer* imply these are the sole province of females. One lawyer tells an endearing story that shows just how far this country has come. Her kindergartner came home one day beaming. "Good news, Mom!" he said. "I found out today guys can be lawyers!"

So remember that he may be a day care provider, she a heliarc welder. She may be the boss; he may be the secretary. (And nobody send *anybody* for coffee: it's just too risky.) Here's some suggested language for writing inoffensively about jobs:

No	Yes
chairman	chair, chairperson
Men Working	Work in Progress
repairman	service representative, technician
salesman	salesperson
spokesman	spokesperson

Speaking of jobs, be aware that the word *employee* has come under fire from the thought police recently. They think it has a demeaning sound and prefer more euphemistic terms, such as *staff, staff member, workers,* or *people.* Ironically, the word *employee* itself was originally a euphemism for the word *servant.* And so we move onward, though the direction of our progress may be in doubt.

■ **Gender: vocabulary.** Some feminists dislike words that reflect, or appear to reflect, historical masculine dominance. If you can do so without its being so obvious as to offend nonfeminists, substitute

workhours	for	man-hours
courageously	for	manfully
face to face	for	man to man
resources	for	manpower
synthetic	for	manmade

| the human race | for | mankind |
| operating | for | manning |

I have a little trouble with this category, and so do some other readers. It seems so—well, small. And being told a word is off limits smacks of censorship. So again, try to make your substitutions unobtrusive. Above all, don't go radical and start writing about *herstory, woman-ual,* and *perone* (*per + one:* not *son*—guess why). That's nonsense that doesn't advance anybody's interests. Besides, these words are derivatively unsound.

■ **Gender: names.** Many names can belong to a person of either sex. For some reason, their owners feel you should know their gender intuitively, and they tend to be humorless and unhelpful about the issue. So, to avoid offending when you must write "Dear Mr." or "Dear Ms." to Lee, Campbell, Cameron, or J. B., hustle around and find out whether it's a boy or a girl. I usually call up on some pretext or other: whoever answers the phone usually gives it away without being asked. Or you can ask.

Of course, if you have a direct-mail list of 1,000 customers, this doesn't work. In such cases, you're better off with "Dear Lee Rogers" or "Dear M. S. Jones." "Dear Sir or Madam" works under some circumstances, but it has a legalistic flavor that may not suit your text.

While I'm at it, don't be too quick to get on a first-name basis. Older people, especially, may view this as just plain rude. Know what? I agree. Especially as I hurtle toward oldpersonhood.

■ **Racial or ethnic group.** I try to avoid labeling, in honor of the fact that we are all primarily people, and also because labels change so fast. Americans who not long ago asked to be called Black rather than Negro now prefer African American to Black. I'm not being fresh: this is their perfect right, but it's honestly hard to keep up. Besides, I'm in favor of ignoring the issue in the hope it'll go away. People, can't we all just get along? For the record, here's what's inoffensive in America today; don't hold me to it tomorrow:

- People of Spanish/American descent prefer to be called Hispanic.
- People of Latin-American descent prefer Latino.
- People of Mexican/Hispanic descent may prefer Chicano. Some dislike it.
- People of African descent prefer African American.
- People of Oriental descent prefer Asian American.
- Our indigenous population chooses Native American or Native American Indian.
- Tiger Woods is Afroamerasian. Or one fantastic golfer.

Watch out for racial or ethnic expressions that may wound or insult. In conversation you may not realize your mistake until too late, and people tend to make allowances and accept a sincere apology. But in writing there are few excuses. And there is no excuse at all for the woman in whose prepared speech as part of a school building dedication I heard, with disbelief, "I didn't think we had a Chinaman's chance in hell of getting the building finished by May." Say—shouldn't that be "Chinaperson's"? Whatever, her largely Asian and Asian American student audience collectively gave, to put it mildly, a sharp intake of breath. On their behalf, so did the rest of us.

Guard against making assumptions in your writing that exclude or simply don't apply to certain groups. The *Boston Globe*'s use of the expression "bled white by war," for example, was criticized in a letter to the editor, because many Americans don't get white when they bleed. I've heard "tickled pink" faulted for the same reason: not everyone's pink, tickled or not. Supersensitive? You bet. Worth honoring? You bet your life. Especially if you're trying to slip through like a liquid.

■ **Designations that highlight age.** *Kids, teens, elders,* and *seniors* are labels that can offend members of those groups also. Not to mention mislabeled nonmembers: it can be dangerous to make assumptions in this context. A friend who markets a highly competitive sports software product was wining and dining four industry principals, men in their early 30s. She's 62, but hardly looks it; she's vivacious and enormously attractive for any age. Cocktails and witty conversation flowed, she was persuasive and charming, the young men responded, and she was expecting to close the deal by dessert, when the waitress asked her, "Would you like to see the senior citizens' menu?" My friend didn't lose the business as a result, but she did lose face, and the waitress lost a tip. Don't make such a howler in writing. Think twice, print once.

■ **Terms that pertain to physical impairment.** My recommendation is to check with the person or group in question. Most are very specific about what they wish to be called. People who have hearing problems, for example, prefer to be known as "hearing impaired people and the deaf," referring, respectively, to those with a lesser or more profound hearing loss. Descriptive terms for many conditions have given way to scientific or medical terms: a person who was called Mongoloid a generation ago is more aptly referred to today as a person with Down or Down's Syndrome. Note also a tendency to label a disease, condition, or injury, rather than a person: hence, "He has mental retardation" rather than "He is retarded."

If you didn't know all this before, you're probably trembling. Join the club (open to everyone). Yes, it's a minefield out there, and we must tread carefully. Don't tell anyone, but occasionally I wish I'd lived in the Bad Old Days, when you automatically called someone with a glass eye Squinty. Sort of cleared the air. My father knew a man everybody called Charley Go Hump because he ended each sentence with "hump." Definitely not a politically correct name, but Dad said Charley didn't seem to mind: he realized the intent was humorous and affectionate. That's probably the heart of the issue: you need to be sure you'll come across as you intend. Maybe we don't know each other well enough nowadays to risk it—well, not in writing, anyway.

◼ THE BOTTOM LINE ◼

- **Write sensitively to avoid offending around gender issues:**
  - **titles and pronouns**
  - **occupations and positions**
  - **vocabulary choices**
  - **names**
- **Avoid discriminating by racial or ethnic group.**
- **Avoid labels that highlight age.**
- **Use appropriate language for physical impairments.**

CHAPTER 15

Have I Maintained the Subject-Verb Connection?

Here's an incredibly easy way to help ensure that your prose communicates. Be certain your subjects stay as close to their verbs as possible without making your sentences sound weird or stilted. Thus *office equipment remains, John was sent, vacations are, the vice president announced,* etc. Not *the vice president, perhaps unduly influenced by his assistant, with whom he was having an extraoffice romance, announced . . .* You'll lose your readers as you saunter toward the action, your verb. They may never find out *what* the vice president did, other than canoodle with a coworker, and they may not care. That's a chance you cannot afford to take. Don't separate subjects and verbs unless you have to, and if you have to, make the split as small as possible.

One way to remember to practice this rule is to think of the two parts of speech as the two halves of a seat belt: buckle up for safety. As you write and when you edit, watch for these pairs and try not to separate them any more than you must:

potential split
location

subject ↓ verb
The new *programmer seems* both pleasant and competent.

potential split
location

subject ↓ verb
When the meeting ended at noon, *everyone felt* encouraged by the progress we'd made.

Especially in the kind of information-intensive writing you do, it's tempting to insert another fact, add another descriptive phrase, include modifiers in the name of caution. Tempting, and awfully easy, too, thanks to the word processor. But overenthusiastically practicing this technique tends to clog the works. When you separate the subject, the initiator in your sentence, from its action, the verb, a sentence emerges that's likely to be confusing, sometimes even ungrammatical. For example:

The new regulation replacing the older ones referring to formica counters the principles of free enterprise.

Anyone besides me misread the sentence, if only briefly, as discussing formica counters? As I've said before, it isn't nice to mislead your reader. Here's another:

Our *president,* with his three vice presidents, and thanks to his able board of directors, *are prepared* to carry this merger forward.

Doubtless the writer would never have said in cold blood, "Our president are. . . ." But as he or she added bits of information, the subject became separated from its verb so widely, and so many bodies got into the act, that it was easy to misconstrue the subject as plural. As a result, our writer wound up not only creating a sprawling, unclear sentence but committing a grammatical error (see Chapter 16 on agreement). All that information can certainly be included if it's important—but it needs to be repackaged:

> Thanks to encouragement from the board of directors and his three vice presidents, the *president is prepared* to carry this merger forward.

or perhaps

> Thanks to encouragement from the board of directors, *the president and his three vice presidents are prepared* to carry this merger forward.

The moral is simple. The more material you compress into the subject-verb cranny, the more likely you are to forget just what your subject *is.* Keep the cranny narrow, the way crannies are supposed to be.

I'm not saying you should never put a modifying clause between your subject and verb. Variety demands it, as does the need to get a lot of information across efficiently. For instance:

> The *manager* who asked for time off *has been fired.*

> *Beth Piper,* taking the annual income projections in turn, *explained* how they had been developed.

No confusion is likely. Nor am I talking about inserting an adverb where it falls naturally:

> *Brian* simply *forgot* that the meeting had been
> rescheduled.

Trying to put *simply* somewhere else (Brian forgot *simply? Simply* Brian forgot? Brian is simple?) to satisfy the rule spoils the sentence while it clouds meaning. That's the worst of both worlds. No, I'm talking big, ugly splits. To the extent you're dealing with complex material, and if you've inserted more than one modifier between subject and verb, you should consider revising: you may be headed for trouble. Here's another example:

> The Bostech *customer service rep,* whether through
> slow call answering, poor listening skills, or inat-
> tention to detail, sometimes *annoy* customers.

In this case, "customer service rep" refers to Bostech reps as a whole or group; with that mindset, and given the wide split before the verb, the writer understandably forgot having written *rep,* not *reps.*

Understandably, but not excusably. You're responsible for your work. That means rereading, and possibly rewriting, to maintain the connection between the actor and the action. I check my copy, especially if my subject is complex or I sense that the writing lacks clarity or grace, to see whether sentence subjects and verbs are sticking together. The more subject-verb pairs I can identify, the more I admire myself. For example, this chapter has sent my self-esteem sky-high. Although I admit to editing and a certain degree of low cunning, you're reading a paragraph that contains six pairs of subjects and verbs in the main part of each sentence—*you're respon-sible, that means, I check, I admire, chapter has sent,* and *you're reading*—and seven more in clauses: *maintain the connection, subject is, I sense, writing lacks, subjects and verbs are, I can identify,* and *I admit.*

You can see for yourself that I've done the same thing pretty consistently throughout the chapter and in fact throughout the book. Like Brooke Shields with her Calvin Klein jeans, I try to let nothing, absolutely noth-ing, come between my subjects and my verbs. See that you do the same.

▣ THE BOTTOM LINE ▣

▪ **Keep your subject and verb connected closely if you can**

> **to maximize clarity**
> **to minimize mistakes**

CHAPTER 16

Have I Addressed Issues of Agreement?

We've already talked about being sure pronouns agree with their subjects (Chapter 11). But other facets of agreement exist. The principle of agreement also requires that subjects and verbs agree in number: singular noun, singular verb. We say James *was,* James and Theo *were.* We say *he is, I was.* These forms are usually correct, but not always. In fact, the whole area is not always that easy to navigate. You can't always tell whether your subject is really a singular or a plural, and even if you know it's singular, your verbs may behave differently under certain conditions. Be careful. Remember, discriminating people may be watching you. (It's my *job* to make you paranoid. Paranoid is just another word for highly aware.) High spots follow where you can pick up a friend or an enemy, depending on whether you're doing things right or wrong. Here are some handy rules to help you over the rough places:

■ *As well as, in addition to,* **and** *with.* These words don't create plural subjects, so the verb stays singular:

Mark, as well as Susan, *is attending* the conference in Dallas.

Estelle, with her four clients, *has reserved* the board room until 6:00 P.M.

In fact, if you bracket part of a group in commas, even with *and,* you've lost them as part of your subject. By using those commas, you identify those people, places, or things as incidental (see use of the comma in Chapter 17):

Jim, and the rest of the board as well, *is* staying at the Ramada Inn.

Sarah, not to mention her three clients, *is* furious at being kept waiting.

If the "extras" in commas are important enough to be part of the subject, then rewrite the sentence to include them: Jim and the rest of the board are staying, Sarah and her three clients are furious.

■ **Rule with *or* and *nor*.** If the parts of a compound subject are joined by *or* or *nor,* the verb agrees with the subject closest to it:

Neither Reed nor his partners *understand* the technology they purchased.

The attorneys or the boss himself *plans* to view the signing.

■ **Group or collective nouns.** Problems arise with "group" or collective nouns: Do we say "The staff *is*" or "the staff *are*"? "Management *is*" or "management *are*"? Surprisingly, the answer is yes and no. The rule is that when the word in question is being considered as a whole, we use a singular verb; when the word identifies things or people considered severally or as individuals, we use a plural one. In the following example, the staff operates as a unified group:

> The staff *is* opposed to a four-day, ten-hour work week.

In the example below, on the other hand, they are operating individually:

> The staff *are* bringing their daughters to work.

Note that you cannot recast *staff* in the singular in that sentence even if you want to without running into a significant problem. The staff is bringing its daughter?

> Management *has offered* a generous severance package.

> Management *have revealed* hidden abilities in the talent show auditions.

Again, in most cases, if you're uncomfortable with the verb, you can easily rewrite:

> The group *has/have* revealed *its/their* compassionate side in the recent dispute.

> The group revealed a compassionate side in the recent dispute.

Among collective nouns, a few special cases exist that are worth mentioning:

-**Majority** and **percentage** are singular or plural depending on whether the collection is singular or plural:

> A majority of *us are* voting against going public.

> A large percentage of the town's *population is* Republican.

-*A* **number** of industrialists *are,* but *the* **number** of industrialists *is.*

English sure is fun! A style manual or grammar handbook will help with a lot of these: *Words into Type* is particularly good.

▢ **Plural subjects treated as single nouns.** I suspect you know this convention and follow it automatically. When you are characterizing an amount of something, as distinguished from the several items involved—be it time, money, unit of measure, or people—you are correct in using a singular verb. The following sentences are therefore just right as they stand:

> *Five hours* without a break *seems* too long for any seminar.

> I asked for *10 customer service reps,* which *was* probably more than we needed.

> *Eighteen miles* is too far from Route 95 for a satellite office.

The recorded voice that tells me when I'm telephone banking that one hundred dollars have been transferred from my account to my son's account grates on me like screeching chalk: it's no use to scream into the phone, "Has been! has been!" She can't hear me. But it's a mistake, and other customers of my bank have mentioned it.

■ **Words that trip some of the people some of the time.** Don't get stuck with an amateur writer label by getting any of these wrong. The following words always take singular verbs:

> **anybody, anyone** *is* . . .
> **each** (of us, of them) *shows* . . .
> **either, neither** (of the offices) *connects* . . .
> **every** (manager and staff member) *remembers* . . .
> **everybody, everyone** *asks* . . .
> **somebody, someone** *obliges* . . .
> **nobody, no one** *compares* . . .

None (of a group of countable persons or things) takes a singular verb if you mean *not one single one.* For example:

> We tested 19 applicants, but none *was* as skilled as Martha.
>
> I tried all the Xerox machines, but none *is* in working order.

And **none** is singular when it refers to a single, uncountable noun:

> None of the *software works* on this machine.
>
> None of the small business *market has* defected to our competition.

None is plural, however, when you mean *not any:*

> I've asked around, but none of our salespeople
> *are* going to Detroit.

> None of us *were* eager to hear about fourth-quar-
> ter earnings.

You may have heard a rule that *none* is always a con-
traction of *no one* and must therefore always take a singular verb. This is one of those rules that come (not
comes: see below) out of nowhere, like the suburban myth
of the razor blade in the Hallowe'en apple. No case of an
apple with a razor blade in it has ever been documented,
but the story spread like kudzu. Same with this *none* habit.
All the authorities are with you on this one, so go ahead
and fight back if your boss challenges you. Produce any
reputable dictionary—an *American Heritage,* for example, or a *Merriam-Webster*—and you'll find the same call.
Show the Big Burrito. Case closed.

▪ **Just one of those things.** The expression "one of
those people who" or "one of those things that" is a useful phrase with a pleasantly conversational ring to it. Be
sure, however, that you are not tricked into thinking the
verb that follows should be singular, modifying *one.* It is
plural, modifying the person or thing, like this:

> Runner Alberto Salazar, on a Boston Marathon
> defeat: "It's just one of those things that *happen.*"

> Katherine Graham, former publisher of the *Wash-
> ington Post*, in her memoir: "Dad wrote me . . .
> that he had had one of those lucky breaks that
> sometimes *occur.*"

To see that the *that* clause in each case modifies the object of the preposition *of* (*things* and *breaks*, in these examples), rather than *one*, just invert the sentence order, which makes the logic clear:

> Of those *things that happen,* this is just one.

> Of those *lucky breaks that sometimes occur,* he had had one.

Yes, it's a small point. But the effect you create with your writing is composed of a number of small points, any of which could be the very thing that happens to bother your discriminating reader. Here are two more examples that demonstrate why the plural is virtually always the correct choice after *one of:*

> She is one of those people who really *enjoy* managing.

> Of those people who really *enjoy* managing, she is one.

> I am one of those investors who *are* comfortable with moderate risk.

> Of those investors who *are* comfortable, . . . I am one.

If you're not convinced and still feel uneasy with the plural verb, or if someone to whom you report hassles you about it, remember that no one is making you use the construction. To slip through without offending, simply rewrite:

It's one of those things that can happen to anyone.

Dad . . . had the kind of lucky break that some-times occurs.

She is among those people who really enjoy man-aging.

As an investor I am comfortable with moderate risk.

▪ **Before you throw in the towel, consult your dictio-nary.** A good dictionary can help you with issues of agreement, by designating a word as a collective noun that follows the rule for collective nouns given above, or by describing its idiosyncratic pattern. Dictionary exam-ples are also helpful. Here's part of the definition of "pol-itics" in my *American Heritage Dictionary:*

> . . . 2. *(used with a sing. or pl. verb.) a.* The activities or affairs engaged in by a government, politician, or political party: *"All politics is local"* (Thomas P. O'Neill, Jr.). *"Politics have appealed to me since I was at Oxford because they are exciting morning, noon, and night"* (Jef-frey Archer). . . .

The entry also includes a usage note that suggests ways to determine whether politics should take a singular or plural verb—in all, as thorough a treatment of the sit-uation as you could wish.

▪ **A word about the subjunctive mood.** *Judith be? I were?* out of context, these sound like peculiarly virulent cases of subject-verb disagreement. Yet you've heard, read, and said them before. These are examples of the subjunctive mood, which causes verbs to behave differently from their usual selves.

In the 18th century, when Patrick Henry declaimed, "If *this be* treason, make the most of it," the subjunctive mood was quite common. Though we don't employ it often today, it has its moments. You've been using it automatically since you were in grade school, but it's useful to know the underlying rationale, should you or a colleague experience a dark night of the subjunctive soul. Two primary reasons exist today for using the subjunctive:

1. Use the subjunctive mood with verbs of commanding or requesting:

   > Edward requested that *Judith and Ron be* ready to fly at a moment's notice.

   > I demand that *Jonathan return* every penny he stole.

   > I ask that *he remember* who gave him his start in this company.

2. Use the subjunctive to express a condition contrary to fact:

   > If *I were* sure he would retain all our staff, I'd gladly sell the shop.

   > If *she were* a kind person, I'd ask for help, but she's most unfeeling.

   > I'd help you if *it were* possible. (But it isn't.)

Do not, however, use the subjunctive for unknown outcomes or simple conditional sentences:

No: John asked if *I were* planning to join them.
Yes: John asked if *I was* going to join them.

No: Howard looked out to see if the *plane were* on the runway.
Yes: Howard looked out to see if the *plane was* on the runway.

To the well informed, you will sound incorrect; to the uninformed, like a smart aleck.

One final subjunctive-related issue. Subjunctive verbs describing a condition contrary to fact *in the past* look just like indicatives, our ordinary verbs, so we wouldn't need to discuss them at all except that for some reason people think the subjunctive is expressed *would have:*

No: If he *would have told* me, I would have changed . . .
Yes: If he *had told* me, I would have changed the prices immediately.

No: If I *would have known* you were job-hunting, I would have . . .
Yes: If I *had known* you were job-hunting, I would have promoted you immediately.

Maybe the *would have* in the second part of the sentence inspires some people to write *would have* in the first half: perhaps it's an effort to balance the two parts of the sentence and effect parallelism, but it's incorrect. You are *never* justified in writing *would have . . . would have.*

Erase it from your mental hard disk in favor of the proper verb construction *had . . . would have*.

That's about it, except for a few idiomatic phrases, such as "come what may" and "so be it." The subjunctive is increasingly rarely used today. But it's correct in these situations, and it lends a little elegance to your prose.

If you are unsure where the battle lines should be drawn on agreement, these rules should help you over the rough spots.

�«ͺ THE BOTTOM LINE ◄

Avoid problems with agreement by following some important rules:

- *As well as*, *with*, **and** *in addition to* **don't create plural subjects.**
- **When** *or* **or** *nor* **links two or more subjects, the verb agrees with the subject closest to it.**
- **Miles, dollars, hours, etc., discussed** *as amounts* **take singular verbs.**
- **Watch for words that can trip you:** *each*, *everyone*, **etc., take singular verbs.**
- **It's "one of those people who** *are***."**
- **Consult your dictionary.**
- **Use the subjunctive mood primarily in two situations.**

CHAPTER 17

Have I Used Punctuation as a Guide to Meaning?

Here are the most important rules of punctuation as applied to business writing. If you follow them, you're unlikely to be misunderstood, and you won't vex people who like to see things done right. These are almost as inflexible as grammar rules. They shouldn't be broken by mistake or for no reason: to make a convention effective and its meaning therefore unambiguous, everybody has to observe it.

Having delivered myself of that weighty pronouncement, I hasten to add that sometimes you need to break a rule to avoid a misunderstanding or misreading of your sentence. After all, the rules were devised to aid communication, not hinder it. But in either case, you're better off knowing what they are.

I've listed the marks of which you should be most aware and the ways to use them—or not use them—so you'll be correct and clear. If you want more detail, see

Kate Turabian's *Manual for Writers*, referenced in the back of this book.

■ **The comma (,)**

The mark you'll need most frequently. Also the most frequently overused, to bad effect. The four major reasons for using the comma follow. There are others, certainly, but be attentive to these four and you'll strongly enhance your readability.

1. To distinguish items in a series of things or descriptive terms:

   > I met with Sam, Jane, and Thomas this morning.

   > She is smart, capable, and well informed.

   If you learned in school that you may drop the final comma, please get over it. This comma is the one that ensures you will not be misunderstood: it prevents misreading the last two items as a unit. Sometimes known as the serial comma, it's the choice of every good style manual going. Peter Lynch uses it, too. Here's a sentence from *One Up on Wall Street*:

   > Another stock I'd avoid is a stock in a company that's been touted as the next IBM, the next McDonald's, the next Intel, or the next Disney, etc.

   I'll take his word for it about the stocks, but I know his punctuation is perfect.

   Here's a line from an apocryphal will, drafted by a lawyer presumably since disbarred:

> I hereby do give, bequeath, and devise my entire estate of $6,000,000 to be shared in equal amounts by my children Tom, Paul and Lily.

Most of us would assume that means $2 million per child. But because there is no comma between the names Paul and Lily, Tom argued—successfully, so says the story—that his father's intent was to leave half of the $6 million to him, and half to Paul and Lily, giving him $3 million and each of them a paltry $1.5 million. It's a safe bet that Christmas was never the same for Tom and his siblings after that. Let's hope the extra million was worth it to him. Even if the story's not true, it's a great example of the power of punctuation and its capacity to render fine shades of meaning.

2. To set off an introductory clause of more than two or three words:

> To match our competitors' strength, we must market more aggressively.

> Watching our account executive's presentation, I was impressed by her knowledge.

You may omit the comma, though you don't have to, after a very short phrase:

> In 1990 First United Bank called Porter-Acheson's commercial loans.

3. To separate independent clauses (same thing as two complete sentences, each with a subject and a verb) joined by *and, but, for, nor, so,* or *or:*

> I wish you could be with us, *but* I understand your reasons for refusing.

> We enjoyed visiting Parker Broadcasting, *and* we're impressed by your digitized telecasting capabilities.

Note that you can't leave out *but, and,* or another conjunction and simply connect with the comma. This is technically known as a run-on sentence or comma splice:

> No: Donna is invaluable, she helps with everything from bookkeeping to sorting coins.

Note also that you can*not* use a comma between two clauses complete with subject and verb and connected with *however, moreover, therefore, otherwise,* or *thus:* these are *not the same* as *and, but,* and the others above. They are adverbs, and they signal a break that requires a semicolon:

> No: I wanted you to join us, however, I understand why you can't make it.
>
> Yes: I wanted you to join us; however, I understand . . .

4. To bracket certain "by the way" information (the sentence may need this information but can structurally stand without it):

> You were there, *in fact,* on the day we signed the contract with Wiggins.

> I asked you on Wednesday, *John,* to return the training video series.

Thursday, *April 23, 1991,* was the date, *also,* of the TriCo, *Inc.,* annual meeting.

I supplied paper, pens, *etc., i.e.,* all the materials needed for the class.

Note that such words and information, including *Inc.,* the year, and all those little Latin abbreviations—*i.e., e.g., etc.—* are *bracketed at either end* by commas (unless they end a sentence and are followed by appropriate end punctuation). Don't stop with just one unless you're at the beginning or end of a sentence:

Yes:	We were able, moreover, to capture market share in both quarters.
Yes:	Moreover, we were able to capture market share in both quarters.
No:	We were able, moreover to capture market share in both quarters.
No:	We were able moreover, to capture market share in both quarters.

Remember that you are excerpting the "by the way" word or additional information: you demonstrate that by hooking the pair of commas around it.

Note: Occasionally (don't take this as a license to start inserting commas everywhere) you may need to insert a comma to prevent a misreading. The following sentence from a recent newspaper editorial should have had one:

The president is more confident about the regulatory uses of government, having proposed a consumers' bill of rights on managed care and flirting with a minimum wage hike.

A comma after "care" would have prevented my first reading of the line as "a bill of rights on managed care and flirting." And in the following sentence:

> I announced to Rogers that I had examined his
> records and called the auditors.

Again a comma is needed to prevent ambiguity. If I told Rogers that I had both examined the records and called the auditors, no punctuation is necessary, as "called the auditors" is not an independent sentence. However, if the meaning of the sentence is that I first told Rogers, then called the auditors, a comma after records is necessary and justified:

> I announced to Rogers that I had examined his
> records, and called the auditors.

That should honestly do it. If you stick with these reasons to use commas, you'll most likely blow through in style. Reasons *not* to insert a comma include sensing a pause in mid-sentence (the ill-considered "breath comma") or simply a long sentence (the worse-considered "death comma"—death, that is, to your image as a writer in control).

▪ The colon (:)
A colon serves two principal functions:

1. To open a business letter.

   Dear John:

2. To indicate that an explanation, a list, or fuller detail follows. It's like a more formal dash.

Mr. Pritzer, the current CEO, named three objectives: to make money, to expand operations, and to restore the firm's good name.

There's no need to restrict coverage by price: consultants should continue to offer both low-cost and high-cost plans.

For example: (1) the lifetime maximum plan; (2) the daily maximum plan; and (3) the modified comprehensive plan

Note: Avoid interrupting running copy (sentences in paragraphs) with a colon. That means do *not* use it like a little trumpet, ta da, in the middle of your sentence:

No: I'd like everyone to bring: a calendar, a monthly work update, and a tentative schedule for next month.

Always complete your sentence before you insert the colon (as I did this one):

Yes: I'd like everyone to bring the following items: a calendar . . .

Yes: I'd like everyone to bring a calendar . . .

■ The dash (—)(–)

The em dash—, on your computer keyboard, is used to

1. express a sharp break in thought:

But to embezzle from the poorest of her clients—can you believe it?

2. introduce detail about foregoing material, like a less formal colon:

> We've identified three possible locations for the headquarters—Chicago, Atlanta, and Durham.

3. add information that might also be bracketed by commas or parentheses:

> The building was slated to be demolished—on May 15, in fact—when an offer came in from Whitman in Los Angeles.

When using dashes in this way, be sure you remember to put them in pairs:

No: She turned away—she obviously didn't want to speak and made her way to a side exit.

Yes: She turned away—she obviously didn't want to speak—and made her way to the side exit.

The en dash (–) is half the length of the em dash in printing. It indicates a range of numbers, dates, times, and the like:

> 1–100, January 20–25, 1998–99, 9:00–5:00

▪ **The hyphen (-)**

I've said punctuation helps clarify meaning. Many people don't understand the principle of hyphenation. Hyphens exist for a very specific purpose: they help show the relationships between words. Consider these two sentence, for example (artfully contrived to prove my point):

The customer ordered twenty three quarter inch
sheets of plywood.

Please deliver ninety five hundred dollar bills.

Where you put the hyphen or hyphens matters a lot. In
the first sentence, as you can see, *Twenty-three sheets,*
each *a quarter of an inch* thick, is quite different from
twenty sheets, each *three-quarters of an inch* thick.
Depending on where you put the hyphens, you'll get a satisfied customer or a displeased and puzzled one. In the
second, ninety-five bills, each worth one hundred dollars?
or ninety-five hundred bills worth one dollar each? The
delivery man wants to know whether to ride his bike or get
out the truck. Here's how to hyphenate in each case:

> . . . ninety-five hundred-dollar bills
> . . . ninety-five hundred dollar bills

In the following headline and church bulletin item,
which are grammar-industry classics, one missing
hyphen in each case has created a major confusion of
meaning:

> Squad Helps Dog Bite Victim

> The ladies of the church have cast off clothing
> of every kind in the parish basement.

While such faux pas may be highly amusing, especially to collectors of bloopers in communications, bear
in mind that your boss may not find them funny in your
writing.

Here are a very few principles that will cover the
greater part of hyphen usage:

1. Use your dictionary. It lists an amazing number of compounds—*hyphenated:* long-term, self-right-eous, one-half; *closed position:* longtime, firsthand, reorder, multinational, workforce; *open position:* growth industry, circuit board, cross section.

2. Use a hyphen to **join a descriptive pair or series of words preceding the noun** they describe. These are usually temporary constructions and the form is very familiar:

   tax-deductible interest, fast-paced presentation

   There's a reason for this. Take the phrase "odd looking glass," for example. Is it a looking glass that's odd? or a glass that is odd looking? "Top flight industry," "level premium method," and "fast moving truck" belong in the same category. The convention of hyphenating says that leaving them open (unhyphenated) means the last two words are described by the first; hyphenating the first two leaves no doubt they are a pair describing the third.

   However, when the descriptive words *follow* the noun they modify, there's little chance of confusion:

   the interest is tax deductible

   the presentation seemed fast paced

   When using familiar pairs of words such as *nursing home* or *interest rate* as descriptive phrases, you don't need the hyphen, though it's not incorrect: nursing home costs, interest rate hikes.

3. There's an exception to Rule 2: **you need not hyphenate after -*ly* adverbs**, such as *chemically*, *wholly*, *attractively*, nor the familiar adverb *very*. Because their appearance indicates their function in the sentence, confusion is unlikely.

> a wholly owned subsidiary; a clearly advantageous strategy; a very good idea

Again, I'm hitting high spots. These principles will get you most of the way. If you want more, the last time I looked *The Chicago Manual of Style* had three pages of running text and a *thirteen-page* chart devoted to using hyphens. Enjoy.

■ The apostrophe (')

This isn't hard. Yet since people get their knickers in a twist about it, let's get it right the first time. The apostrophe is used to indicate two scenarios:

1. Possession.

Single noun or name	Possessive: add ('s)
company	company's
Joan	Joan's
business	business's
Charles	Charles's

Now you have two minutes to ventilate and complain that you learned in school to drop the final *s* after a single noun ending in *s*. Some people did teach that, and some learned it. As for me and virtually all the reputable style manuals, we don't give you even the option. Why? because the consistent 's form is less likely to be misunderstood. And because it is what most people actually say when they pronounce a possessive. Try pronouncing it: "Lewis's fund." As opposed to, say, "the Lewis Fund."

Exceptions: Ancient Greek and Biblical names, such as Achilles and Moses, and *for goodness'* or *conscience' sake.*

Some people complain that the rule results in some unwieldy constructions, such as "Massachusetts's industry." All right, but assuming you have more resources than dumb, driven cattle, you can simply write around it: "The industry of Massachusetts" or simply "Massachusetts industry" (like "U.S. industry") is accurate and euphonious. A woman named Alexis in one of my seminars told us her fourth-grade teacher had been unequivocal about the possessive of her name, *'s:* it was "*Alexis's* boots," not *Alexis'.* I could tell the class was more impressed by this story than by anything I'd said on the subject.

Plural noun ending in s	Add (')
businesses	businesses'
professors	professors'
taxes	taxes'
Joneses (Mr. and Mrs. together)	Joneses'

Plural noun not ending in s	Add ('s)
women	women's
people	people's
courts-martial	courts-martial's
alumni	alumni's

If the apostrophe denotes possession, in referring to a company's balance sheet, why do we say *its,* rather than *it's,* balance sheet? I noted this in Chapter 11 on pronouns—it's because all the pronouns, being a zillion years old, do their own thing. They're irregular and *never* take a possessive apostrophe. That's right, never. It's comforting. Write, *his, hers, yours, its, ours, theirs, whose.*

2. Omission. An apostrophe can also mean a letter has been left out:

> I can't, she didn't, I'm, they're, it's (for *it is* or *it has*), the '90s

Be sure to put the apostrophe where the missing letter would have gone. If you have trouble with this, your spell checker is very clear about it, which leaves no excuse for writing *does'nt* or *its'.*

The convention of using *'s* to indicate the plural of abbreviations and numbers is headed the way of the lava lamp: kind of retro, a period piece, for looking at, not for serious use. It's too easily mistaken for a possessive. Write simply

> Local YMCAs, ATMs; the 1990s, the '80s

Exceptions: If your abbreviation contains more than one period, if it ends in an *s,* or if a simple *s* could otherwise cause confusion, add *'s:*

She holds two *M.A.'s* from the University of Michigan.

Her memos usually represent *SOS's.*

The new interns are minding their *p's* and *q's.*

■ **The period (.)**

Note in the examples above that most of the abbreviations are without periods, properly called points, in this case, a convention that's becoming increasingly familiar:

NYSE, ROI, CIA, CD-ROM, NAACP, IMF

If your organization prefers to use points with certain acronyms or abbreviations, that's fine: just be sure you communicate this to everyone writing for you and are consistent in your treatment, especially within a piece. If you are writing to an organization that abbreviates its name, do exactly as the organization does, no matter what your own house style.

Periods end sentences and go *inside* quotation marks. you do not need them after items in a vertical list unless one or more items are complete sentences:

In case of fire, follow these steps:
- Dial 911 to report the fire.
- Use stairways, not elevators.
- Leave the building and remain outside

The Royal 500 has three modes
- Ready
- Standby
- Power saver

■ **Quotation marks (" ")**

1. Use quotation marks to enclose someone's exact words:

   Your client then asked me, "Why on earth should I pay Henry?"

2. Use them to introduce an unfamiliar word or phrase:

   "To indemnify" means to protect against damage, loss, or injury.

3. Use them to indicate that something is so-called but phony:

   He offered us a chance to get in on a "sure thing."

The inference in that sentence is that the horse, stock, or whatever is anything *but* sure.

People sometimes have trouble remembering whether to put punctuation inside or outside quotation marks. The problem is complicated if you read books printed in Great Britain or Canada, where the marks go inside or outside, depending on whether they are part of the quoted material or not. For Americans, the system is illogical but easy: remember that no matter what logic indicates, **quotation**

marks always go outside periods and commas; otherwise, they go inside or out according to whether the colon, semicolon, question mark, or whatever is part of the quoted material:

> His idea of a "revolving bond fund," quoted in the article "Narrow Rate Spreads," might have been viable when interest rates were high, but I feel it is poorly suited to today's financial environment.

> Why did you quote his article, "Narrow Rate Spreads"? I have investigated the concept of a "revolving bond fund": it offers no potential for our market today.

Why do periods and commas always go inside quotation marks? A story, possibly apocryphal, explains why and may help you remember where they belong. Before the invention of automatic typesetting, printers discovered that if they set type with a quotation mark followed by a period or a comma, like this—(".)—these very small punctuation marks tended to get knocked off the end of the line of type. Accordingly, they began putting the periods and commas safely *in*side the quotation marks, where they remain to this day.

Don't overuse quotation marks. You may enclose an unfamiliar word or phrase in quotation marks the first time you use it. Once you've identified or explained it, however, you don't need to keep wrapping the quotation marks around it. In fact, you shouldn't, because it's distracting and a little annoying.

Speaking of which, I don't think you'd do this, but just in case you're tempted, don't ever use quotation marks, in advertising or elsewhere, to highlight a name or description:

> Jayne's Homemade "Ice Cream"
>
> Visit Dale's showroom and get the "best rates around"!

Although you may be using them as an attention-getting device, like boldface type, it looks entirely too much as if you're using them in the sense of (3) above. As though Jayne is, in fact, making ice cream out of recycled styrofoam and Dale has lousy rates. Once, driving past a mailbox that said "The Holtons," my family and I made rude remarks about who actually could be living there under the alias of Holton. Amelia Earhart? Judge Crater? Evidently not the Holtons.

▓ Single quotation marks (' ')

Some people use these, for no good reason, in place of the double marks. Please don't: they have a very specific function. They serve to enclose another quotation, or a title that would ordinarily be enclosed in quotation marks, within quoted material. Here's an example:

> Mr. Forbes said, "Your article, 'Getting Rich on a Fixed Income,' strained the credulity of the *Forbes* editorial board."

In business writing you're probably not going to need single quotation marks often.

▓ The semicolon (;)

Two very useful functions performed by the semicolon are

1. To connect two complete sentences that are related in thought. You may include a conjunction such as *and* or *but,* but it's not necessary, as it is when a comma is the joining mark:

   > I don't blame you for asking to see the man's identification; he doesn't look like one of our regular couriers.

   > We can take a taxi to the airport early in the afternoon; but I've been wondering if the train wouldn't be a better idea.

   The semicolon makes a break sharper than that of the comma, but not so sharp as that of a period.

2. To divide and clarify a series that contains internal punctuation. The semicolon is an excellent device to avoid confusion in such cases. For example, here's a sentence with a structure particularly familiar from photo captions:

   > Key members of the systems team are shown above. They are, from left, John Erskine, first vice president with overall responsibility for coordinating the effort company-wide, Mary Jane Abdul, systems designer, Susan Atkins, our team leader, Ann Brownell, administrative assistant, and Harry Hartwell, head programmer.

   If you're reading carefully, you can match names and functions. It's easy if you're skimming casually, however, to read "our team leader, Ann Brownell," and so on. To ensure that descriptive information attaches clearly to the person intended, the semicolon functions as a sort of fire-wall, dividing more strongly than the commas:

> . . . John Erskine, first vice president with over-all responsibility for coordinating the effort company-wide; Mary Jane Abdul, systems designer; Susan Atkins, our team leader; Ann Brownell, administrative assistant; and Harry Hartwell, head programmer.

▪ Slash (/)

This mark, also known as a virgule or a solidus, can join two words or phrases with the useful meaning of *this, that,* or *both:*

> Jack Davis functions as our plant manager/pur-chasing agent.

Evidently, since the two functions are not readily blended, Jack operates sometimes as plant manager, sometimes as purchasing agent, and, presumably on bad days, as both. That's a good use for the slash. Don't start slashing around, however; you can overwork this mark by using it as a substitute for a hyphen or the word "and":

> Ilene Farber was named president/CEO of Aitken Industries in May.

Remember that the slash adds that interesting sugges-tion of "or." Ilene isn't president *or* CEO, she's both. So say *president-CEO* or *president and CEO.*

The slash is used perhaps most often in the construc-tion *and/or.* Here's a legitimate use for this one, where either or both is meant:

> As time permits, please show our prospect the
> Data Automation building, the new paint room,
> and/or the automated punch press operation.

Don't get crazy with *and/or,* either: it gets to be a distracting tic in some people's writing. Possibly they think
it covers all contingencies and therefore captures some
sort of quasi-legal high ground. Actually, it's more often
simply tedious. Ask yourself whether *and* or *or* alone
wouldn't be simpler and just as accurate:

> Please bring a copy of your most recent paystub,
> mortgage statement, and/or IRS records for the
> preceding year.

Come on. If you want all three, write *and.* Otherwise,
don't insinuate that some poor soul should go dig them all
out. Write *or.*

■ Parentheses (( ))

Try not to use these if you don't have to. They break
up your line visually, and they tend to imply the information inside is unimportant. Commas work better for material that's closely related to the rest of the sentence:

> No: Our chairman and CEO (Francis Brownell)
> resigned today.
> Yes: Our chairman and CEO, Francis Brownell,
> resigned today.

Punctuate and capitalize with parentheses like this:

> At Feradyne (not to be confused with Teradyne),
> we do only finish work.

I learned double-entry bookkeeping last fall (it isn't hard).

We asked him to give an overview of the proposed system. (He had volunteered to provide one at his expense.)

Don't place a comma or other internal punctuation ahead of a phrase in parentheses:

No: When I arrive, (assuming the plane's on time) I'll go straight to Becq.

Yes: When I arrive (assuming the plane's on time), I'll go. . . .

Yes: We arrived. (The plane was on time.) We went straight. . . .

▪ Brackets ([])

Like the single quotation marks, brackets are second-generation parentheses: that is, they go inside a pair of parentheses if you must excerpt something within the parenthesized material:

Gauchand-Eiger (whose largest plant [see map of facilities, page 14] is in Lausanne) is a major target for takeover by our Swiss subsidiary.

Brackets are also useful if you must interject a comment of your own when quoting someone else's writing or speech:

Gleasman's comments on the Web site follow: The printouts of the Web site have two parts. As the site was designed to be shown on screen [as

> part of the Olympic demo], some printouts appear
> to have text missing.

The word *sic,* Latin for *thus,* means that's the way the person quoted, wrote, or said it. Sort of a mean way of pointing out an error while noting it's not of your doing. It is generally italicized and bracketed:

> This is in fact whitetext [*sic*] that will not appear
> in printouts.

■ **Exclamation point (!)**
Even if you're writing advertising copy, I recommend limiting the use of this mark. Heavily exclamatory writing makes you appear unsophisticated and perhaps overly excitable. Calvin Trillin says it's a bad way of calling attention to your line, like laughing at your own joke.

Punctuation marks are little, but don't think for a minute they're unimportant. They function like street signs along an unfamiliar route. By clarifying meaning and explaining the function of sentence elements, they help your readers remain on course as they negotiate the hills, turns, and straight-aways of your prose.

THE BOTTOM LINE

■ **Use this chapter as your guide to selecting and using punctuation correctly.**

CHAPTER 18

Have I Chosen Concrete Language Whenever Possible?

Don't overuse abstract words. Convenient as they are, they have a big downside. I'm talking about such words as these:

facility	circumstance
performance	relationship
contact	impact
event	equipment
effect	situation
function	result

Navigating the business world, you may have noted a disquieting preference for the general-category or all-purpose word rather than the specific one. What a quick and easy way to drain your writing of color and make it forgettable! What's the reason for this peculiar preference? It may reflect caution, a refusal to get specific and risk one's backside. Or perhaps it's a (faulty) perception that these words are, by their very lack of color, businesslike.

Whatever the cause, it's unattractive and it's information poor. Consider the following sentences:

> Please *contact* me if you have any questions.

> We plan to break ground for the new *facility* in May.

Then compare the punch delivered by

> Please *call me at 203-872-8448* if you have any questions.

> We plan to break ground for the new *performing arts theater* in May.

In a few words, that's the difference between concrete and what I call "covering" language.

Contact and *facility* are examples of covering language. There's no denying such words are useful, because just one will cover a number of possibilities. You can *contact* someone, for example, by many methods: phone, fax, e-mail, and carrier pigeon, to name but a few. And *facility* can describe a multiplex of buildings and structures, from offices to warehouses to lighthouses to phone booths and portable lavatories.

But because they apply in a range of situations, covering words are by nature imprecisely focused. They are abstractions that create little or no visual impression, and therefore they are not memorable. And you are not supposed to substitute them for concrete, specific words. Alas, people do it anyhow. Sometimes they even write "Please *contact* me at 631-7967 if you have any questions." This is not what covering words were designed for.

A covering word such as *event* allows us to describe things that may be dissimilar but that occupy the same position relative to the sense of a sentence. A covering word such as *events* is practically indispensable to describe the disparate items listed below:

> Research indicates that a job change, the birth or death of a child, and a change in health are major *events* that can threaten a marriage.

But I would never, ever, *ever* use the word *event* as a substitute for *marathon,* or *ribbon cutting,* or *cocktail party,* any more than I would describe a *marriage* as a *relationship:*

> The Jewetts are holding an event at the Ritz to commemorate their relationship.

That kind of writing raises more questions than it answers. Focus as sharply as possible on the specifics and be memorable:

> The Jewetts are celebrating their 30th wedding anniversary with an all-night black-tie dinner dance for 200 people at the Ritz.

If the newspaper mentions the possibility of a "precipitation event," do you get a mental picture of what's going to happen? Now if the weatherfolk are considering the possibility of everything from cats and dogs to lemon drops falling from the sky, there's justification for *precipitation,* if not *event:* the word covers a number of conditions. But I'd always prefer to read *rain, snow, sleet,* or *hail.* Not to mention lemon drops. How different and specific are the feelings each of those words evokes! We're creatures of matter and space ourselves, after all, not bodiless abstractions. We yearn for words that engage our senses.

(Same issue, different context: I hate it when a new bride thanks me for my "gift" without naming it specifically. She can't identify a casserole dish? The groom could be in for some bad surprises.)

Even harder on your readers is covering language that yields no clue to the nature of what it's supposed to describe. It covers so many possibilities that it is "spineless": you can't tell whether you're reading good or bad news. For example:

> The new regulation will have a profound *impact* on our revenues.

Impact, my foot. Evidently, somebody stands to make or lose a lot of money. I can think of no reason why the writer should keep readers in the dark as to which. Take your pick:

> The new regulation will *triple* our revenues.

> The new regulation will *devastate* our revenues.

Now that's news you can sink your teeth into. That's good, because business writing is starved for specifics. Whenever it's at all possible, turn those covering words loose in favor of concrete ones. If several different options are possible and you want to leave them all open, then go with covering language. But if you can hone in sharply, you'll create an image in a reader's mind that will linger, prompting, with any luck, the response you want.

Preferring the concrete word may give you another, subliminal advantage. Author and former news commentator Robert MacNeill makes an intriguing point in his autobiography, *Wordstruck*. Most of the abstract words in our language are derivatives of Latin, which, dating from the arrival of Christianity in England at the end of the sixth century, was the language of the church, of thought and knowledge, and of the upper classes. As such, words borrowed from Latin tend to represent abstract concepts. They also tend to be long, because you know the Romans: they took a root, added a bunch of prefixes and suffixes, and voila! *contradistinctively.*

The words derived from Old English, on the other hand, are mostly short, and these "Anglo-Saxon monosyllables" are the language of the concrete: the words for food and shelter, family, the human body. *Mother, father, head, hand, foot, bread, meat, milk, love, home, heart.* These are the words for our basic needs, and they comprise a child's earliest vocabulary, notes MacNeill. He theorizes that when you use these words, you reach people at an emotional as well as a rational level. You make a subliminal appeal to them. That can't be bad for business.

Well, yes, but how can we really pull that off in business writing? By valuing the short word as much as the long one. Just because a word is long doesn't make it impressive: *help* is every bit as good a word as *facilitate.* Also, you just might score subliminal points by putting in a word derived, I mean *got,* from Old or Middle English when you get the chance:

> Roget Systems is the data processing *arm* of the company.

I'm not being frivolous: try it. It certainly can't hurt. And if you check the supreme stylists of the English language—from William "To Be Or Not To Be" Shakespeare to E. B. "Some Pig" White—you're going to be forced to admit that for them, the Anglo-Saxon monosyllables are the words of choice.

⊞ THE BOTTOM LINE ⊞

- **Use concrete, specific language whenever you can.**
- **Use covering, abstract language to refer to dissimilar or unknown elements.**

CHAPTER 19

Have I Been Ambiguous, Illogical, or Off the Wall?

O ne of the most important aspects of business is gaining the confidence of clients, customers, and colleagues. You cannot afford to erode their confidence by making what I call "What th—?" statements— statements that would have caused a 1950s comic book hero to utter that scrupulously clean expletive. Take this sentence, for example, recently gleaned from the front page of my morning paper:

> Funds to renovate the overcrowded, run-down
> building died Wednesday in the Legislature.

Look out for dead funds in the halls of Congress! I'm guessing that for lack of space the original caption, which probably began with "A proposal to renovate" or "A bill for funding," was shortened, with fatal results. You can't afford this kind of careless writing if you want to impress readers. That caption unimpressed me intensely, and my opinion of the newspaper, never high, fell another few points.

Here's how to purge your writing of ambiguous, illogical, and off-the-wall declarations that can hurt you and your organization.

■ **Make pronoun references clear.** Your readers need to know, without having to dig around for it, to what or whom a pronoun refers. In the sentence below, meaning and communication aren't well served because it's impossible to tell whether *she* and *her* refer to Rachel or Anne:

> Originally, Rachel and Anne were scheduled to work together, but when *she* became ill, *she* turned over *her* responsibilities to Ken.

There are at least three possible ways to read the sentence. That's no kindness to the reader. Try

> Originally, Rachel and Anne were scheduled to work together, but when *Anne* became ill, *Rachel* turned over *Anne's* . . .

I'll grant you it isn't elegant, but the meaning is clear. In context you may be able to put it more gracefully:

> Originally, the two colleagues were scheduled to work together, but when *Rachel* became ill, *Anne* turned over *her manager's* . . .

Also, be sure your pronouns refer to an actual name or noun, not to some hazy but unexpressed concept. Look at the following sentence:

> Marshall said he could construct a new stone wall for Regis Corp., but he wouldn't design the building facade: *it* was too difficult for him.

What was too difficult? You cannot point, as you must be able to, to a specific noun for which *it* stands in the sentence. That's because the pronoun refers to nothing solid or explicitly named in the sentence, but, apparently, to the effort to design the facade, or the design, or the creation of the design. In the revision below, *it* clearly stands for the noun *design:*

> . . . but he wouldn't attempt *the design* of the building facade: *it* was too difficult for him.

■ **Avoid incoherent noun references as well.**

> Ms. Keyser operates a *salmon farm, an industry* that appears to have a bright future.

> The new *product,* a petroleum additive, is our *goal* for this quarter.

Salmon *farming* is an industry: a salmon farm is not. And a product design, innovation, production, or rollout may be a goal, but calling a product a goal is vague and illogical.

■ **Be sure your comparisons are matching and finished off.** Remember the wheeze about comparing apples to oranges? It applies importantly in writing. This, for example, is an incoherent comparison:

> My *job* is more difficult than my *manager.*

The items you compare have to match. You must compare job with job: hence, *my manager's, my manager's job,* or *that of my manager.* The same applies in the following sentence:

Our *GNP* is twice as big as *Japan.*

No, it isn't. It's twice as big as *Japan's GNP.* Be sure you're comparing apples to apples.

Your comparisons must also be finished. Here is a sentence containing two comparisons, only one of which is complete:

> The new salesman is *as good* or *better than* his predecessor.

Though I hate to keep saying this, you can't say that. There's no problem with *better than his predecessor.* But *as good his predecessor? as good than his predecessor?* That comparison is incomplete, because it's missing a word:

> The new salesman is as good *as* or better than his predecessor.

Finally, don't write a comparative word such as *better* or *further* without saying, if at all possible, better or further than *what.* I know advertising makes lavish use of this device: the airlines fly you farther, the new detergent gets your wash whiter, and it's better in the Bahamas. But in the overwhelming majority of cases, you should complete the comparison, for the sake of logic and clarity:

> No: Our company offers better benefits.
> Yes: Our company offers better benefits *than the company that has made you an offer.*

> No: Harry's presentation was more convincing.
> Yes: Harry's presentation was more convincing *than Joanne's.*

Don't forget that you as the writer *know* than what or whom; the person to whom you're writing may or may not know; another person who reads your work may very well have no idea. Don't risk it. Besides, finished comparisons just sound better. Better than unfinished ones.

▪ **Put modifying phrases near their subject.** A descriptive phrase tends to attach itself to whatever is closest to it. Consider these two sentences:

> Reynolds suggested that we merge our two companies over cocktails.

> Susan will move into the cubicle next to the refrigerator, which was my original office.

In the first, the phrase *over cocktails* appears to refer to the proposed merger, putting a peculiar slant on the whole idea. In fact, the phrase properly belongs to *Reynolds suggested* and should be placed accordingly. In the second, *which was my original office* suggests by its placement that our writer previously occupied office space in the refrigerator. A minor rearrangement of text will prevent this embarrassing misperception:

> *Over cocktails,* Reynolds suggested that we merge our two companies.

> Susan will move into *my original office,* the cubicle next to the refrigerator.

▪ **Don't mix metaphors.** An alert friend called to report this awe-inspiring gaffe made by a Virginia senator on national television:

> My colleague is leading you through a Byzantine
> thicket of quicksand.

A mixed metaphor is a pileup of two, or in this case three, figures of speech on one another. Byzantine means intricate, sometimes bejeweled. Thickets aren't Byzantine, and they aren't made of quicksand, either. Such bloopers give the impression that a writer is at least partially out of control. Here's another:

> The ship of state is leaping the hurdles of foreign
> tariffs.

Ships sail waves, runners leap hurdles. Ships don't leap hurdles, and the twain shouldn't be meeting in that sentence. And I'm horrified that the following is the work of a school principal:

> The principal is a one-man band who puts out
> fires and maintains his sacred cows.

By all means use metaphors in your writing: business writing, as I've said, is desperate for color. But be careful of such unintended mixing. It may be entertaining, but it makes readers question your reliability, if not your sanity.

■ **Don't dangle participles or modifiers.** The names may sound intimidating, but these are relatively easy to deal with. If you don't deal with them, dangling participles and dangling modifiers can also produce perhaps the most spectacular "what th—"s in the writing business. Here are three examples:

Sputtering, popping, and blowing fuses, the marketing director helplessly watched his presentation self-destruct in the projector.

In day care since the age of two, his parents were prominent attorneys.

Having spent an exciting weekend in Los Angeles, my briefcase was missing.

Though in principle I have nothing against marketing heads popping fuses, parents languishing in day care, and briefcases on weekend escapades, such errors make your writing look less than serious. And writing that's hard to take seriously is not good business writing. These amazing effects are achieved, once again, through location: the modifier, beginning with an *-ing* word if it's a participial phrase, attaches itself to the very first subject it encounters. If that noun is not the real subject of the descriptive phrase, you have a problem—as you can see from the examples above. You have two options for grounding these dangling constructions: (1) Be sure the *real* subject of the phrase is the next noun *after* the comma:

Sputtering, popping, and blowing fuses, *the projector* destroyed the marketing director's presentation.

Or (2) make sure the subject is expressed in the phrase itself, *preceding* the comma:

As *the projector* began sputtering, popping, and blowing fuses, the marketing director helplessly watched it destroy his presentation.

1. In day care since the age of two, *he* was the son of two prominent attorneys.
2. *He* had been in day care since the age of two; his parents were prominent attorneys.

1. Having spent an exciting weekend in Los Angeles, *I* discovered my briefcase was missing.
2. After *I* had spent an exciting weekend in Los Angeles, my briefcase . . .

In the following sentence, the meaning's so clear it may be hard to spot the problem:

Reviewing your proposal, everything has gone wrong.

But the problem exists, and the sentence is off. *Everything* can't review proposals. To eliminate the dangling participle, you must say something along these lines:

1. Reviewing your proposal, *I* have had a series of mishaps.
2. When *I* tried to review your proposal, everything went wrong.

■ **Edit out "no-way" statements.** Finally, don't give readers a reason to respond "No way!" when they read your stuff. It's easy to make no-way statements—if you're writing hastily, editing carelessly, or simply too close to your material. It's hard to believe it, but the following three sentences are the work, respectively, of a magazine reporter, a columnist for a major daily, and an advertising copywriter for a large corporation:

The early years of the magazine were an exciting place to work.

The fiddlehead ferns are past being edible to pick.

Sometimes a once-in-a-lifetime opportunity comes along.

My daughter Sarah, at age 10, read that one over my shoulder and denounced as "weird" the notion that a once-in-a-lifetime event could happen sometimes—once a month, maybe?

It's kind of funny when someone else blows it—but just one of these statements can totally undermine a reader's confidence in you. Read carefully before you print to be sure you haven't said something impossible or ridiculous.

THE BOTTOM LINE

- **Be sure your pronouns refer clearly to their subjects.**
- **Watch incoherent references: a *product* is not a *goal*.**
- **Compare similar items; complete your comparisons.**
- **Put descriptive phrases near their subjects.**
- **Don't mix metaphors.**
- **Don't dangle participles or modifiers.**
- **Never give your reader cause to say "No way!"**

CHAPTER 20

Have I Sweated the Small Stuff?

Iknow I've made this point frequently, but I'm guessing you need to hear it again: It's worth it to sweat the small stuff. Some of the people who read your work will be put off by even the littlest mistakes. In fact, some people evidently go looking for them. A 1994 Dilbert cartoon shows Wally returning Dilbert's report with "a few thousand suggestions" and the following comment: "Of all the pleasures of life, I think I like nit-picking the best." The small stuff is important because it's possible the people you want to impress are people like Wally. The following glitches are small ones indeed, but they can raise a disproportionate amount of complaints when they appear. If discriminating readers get the impression you're careless or ignorant in these small things, they are less likely to trust your message.

▧ **Don't overuse capital letters.** Observe four big rules for the use of capital letters:

1. **Capitalize the proper names** of persons, places, and things, as I hope Mrs. Adams taught you in fourth

grade (dare I hope they're teaching *anything* about correct writing in these last days? The Grammar Goths are over the wall and confusion reigns).

2. **Look in a good style manual** such as *Chicago* or *Words into Type* to get the scoop on particular cases: governmental bodies, regions of the country, etc. It will tell you to capitalize *Northeast* (sales in the Northeast) but not *government* (U.S. government), *English* but not *economics,* and so on.

3. **Observe house style.** Whether you use initial caps for certain words or categories of words—such as the titles of people or divisions in your organization—is to a certain extent a function of your company's style. If there is such a thing, written or unwritten, make yourself familiar with it and use it.

4. **Minimize.** Beyond the first three rules, I'd counsel you to lay the caps on very lightly. Overdone, they tend to make your writing look Victorian or even older. You don't want to be mistaken for a member of the Heaving Bosom School of Writing. This is business writing, and it shouldn't appear frenetic. Also, capitals distract by making your line stutter: the eye is forced up and down, up and down as you read. Here's an excerpt from the United States Constitution, drafted in 1787, that makes heavy use of initial caps:

> Article. IV, Section 1: Full Faith and Credit shall be given in each State to the public Acts,

Records, and judicial Proceedings of every other State.

So goes the entire document: it's like German, with practically every noun capitalized. To the modern American eye, it's odd, possibly even a little breathless. Compare that with an amendment to the same document, proclaimed in 1971:

Amendment XXVI: The right of citizens of the United States, who are 18 years of age or older, shall not be denied or abridged by the United States or any state on account of age.

Very easy on the eyes. What a difference 200 years makes! That's how it's typically done these days.

By the same token, though, easy on the eyes can translate into "doesn't catch one's attention." For this reason, especially if you're a writer of promotional copy, you probably make use of capital letters as well as font treatment, point size, and other techniques to draw your readers' attention and create emphasis:

Be sure to visit our store during our Grand Opening Sale!

I still counsel moderation. Just look at the excerpt from Article IV, above: everything emphasized adds up to nothing emphasized.

■ **Put your words in their proper places.** In general, a word belongs as close as possible to the words with which it's associated. If you observe this maxim, you'll measurably improve the clarity of your writing. Here are four adverbs (words that tell how) that tend to wander when you're not watching closely:

1. **Only.** Many people are careless with *only,* and the results are unsatisfactory. To be sure you're putting it in its proper place, say to yourself, "What is it that's *only?*" A philosopher might say, "In what does the onliness inhere?" Take a look at this example:

   > If you *only* need to write a few checks each week . . .

   What's *only* in this sentence? The word's misplaced, because it isn't a question of only *needing,* as opposed, say, to *wanting.* And it isn't only *to write,* as opposed to *to photograph.*

   The correct answer is, of course, only *a few checks,* as opposed, perhaps, to *a lot:*

   > If you need to write *only* a few checks each week . . .

   Obviously, you can change the meaning of some sentences, depending on where you place *only:*

   > She improved *only* her bookkeeping when her manager complained (she did nothing about her keyboard skills).

   > She improved her bookkeeping *only* when her manager complained (then, and not earlier).

Here's another:

The auditor *only* asked me once for those expense records.

Although the sentence as written focuses attention on the act of asking, it seems clear from the context that the auditor asked *only once*.

2. **Just.** A similar issue. Be sure you place *just* as close as possible to what it modifies. Suppose you need three contracts to fund your payroll:

No: If we could *just* get three contracts, we could meet payroll.

Yes: If we could get *just* three contracts, we could meet payroll.

In this case, you want to emphasize the number, not the act of getting. Compare with the following sentence, in which the emphasis *is* on the act of getting:

If we could *just* get this contract, we could meet payroll.

3. **Even.**

No: You are asked not to *even* touch one of the buttons on the keypad.

Yes: You are asked not to touch *even* one of the buttons . . .

It's clear this is not about touching, as opposed to say bashing. Avoid splitting an infinitive as you zero in on *one,* the real focus of the sentence.

4. **Almost.**

> No: I *almost* contacted every one of the marketing reps.
>
> Yes: I contacted *almost* every one of the marketing reps.

We're creatures of mind and spirit, but we are limited by physical space. And these spatial constraints offer an opportunity to home in very precisely on elements of meaning in our writing. Take advantage of them.

▪ **Treat abbreviations and acronyms correctly.**

First, *identify* abbreviations unless they are as universally understood as, for example, M.D. or U.S. I recommend in most cases giving the full name first, then the abbreviated form in parentheses:

> The North Atlantic Treaty Organization (NATO)
>
> The Division of Youth Services (DYS)

You may then continue to use the abbreviation or acronym as you wish without further identification. You don't have to, of course: you may use the spelled-out version if you prefer it in a particular spot.

I need to get up on my orange crate to make my next pronouncement: I hope you can all hear me. Just because you express an abbreviation in capital letters *does not* necessarily mean that the word or phrase should be capitalized:

> Operational efficiencies are a feature of point-of-sale (POS) terminals.

> We expect to realize a stunning return on investment (ROI) through the merger.

Confusion sometimes arises over whether to put "a" or "an" before an abbreviation. You'll get it right every time if you say the article and the abbreviation aloud. For example:

> Please call Marjorie to find out whether we have an SBANE (pronounced *ess-bane*) meeting.

> We asked you for a SWIFT (pronounced *swift*) transmission.

> This is not an FDIC-insured (*eff-dee-eye-cee*) loan.

> Why is Excelsius still a FORTRAN (*fore-tran*) program?

As I said in Chapter 17 on punctuation, the tendency nowadays is to write abbreviations without periods, or points. Follow your organization's policy; if it's their abbreviation, follow theirs; follow your dictionary; if these guidelines are missing, be consistent in your own writing.

Write out United States as a noun in business copy, rather than using the abbreviations U.S. or USA. As a modifier, U.S. is fine: *U.S. forces in Eastern Europe.*

A word about *versus:* In citing legal cases, the abbreviation for versus is written *v.;* in other uses, if you must abbreviate it—perhaps in a memo subject line—it's abbreviated *vs.*

> Decades ago, in Roe v. Wade. . . .

> The advantages of the digital duplicator vs. the photocopier. . . .

In everyday writing, use *against* or *as opposed to* in preference to v. or vs.

■ **Handle symbols with particular care.** Symbols that may be appropriate for certain other types of writing should not be used in business copy. In strictly mathematical or scientific copy, for example, the symbol % is used; in business copy, use the word *percent* unless you are going to be expressing pages and pages of percentages, as in, for example, an annual report.

Some symbols were used more commonly and with more justification when someone had to pull out an inkwell and a large piece of bird plumage in order to write. That's certainly the mood you create when you use them, and you should be aware of this. Such symbols include a favorite with some people (I have no idea why), the ampersand, or *&*. This mark is a substitute for the word *and.* Once entirely respectable, it looks oddly dated nowadays: along the lines of beginning a letter "Dear Wm" and signing off "Yrs, Chas."

The ampersand is still used today in the names of firms: Callard & Bowser, Standard & Poor; R & D is a standard reference to research and development; and some agencies and businesses still use it when coining department or product names: Fisheries & Game Management, Marketing & Product Development, and the like. But don't use an ampersand in place of "and" unless your organization has created a title or name that includes it (and if they haven't already printed up the letterhead stationery, stop them).

The same goes for #. This symbol for *number* may be used in scientific or mathematical writing, but it is not appropriate as a synonym for number in ordinary business writing. Don't shame your organization by using the symbol this way:

> The # of people insisting on a refund is still very small.

I recently edited a letter for a young executive who referred several times to dollars, which he rendered as "$s." This would be fine if you were writing a note in haste to your spouse: "Stop at the ATM and get me some $s." It is not fine in your writing. Handle money respectfully.

■ **Write out "don't use 'ems."** Like the infamous "no see'ums" of New England, tiny but infuriating biting insects, the "don't use 'ems" can ruin your day. Slap the following phrases into oblivion if you catch them in your work. A grab bag of baddies I've collected over time, these words and phrases may not *always* be incorrect, but they are considered poor usage in certain cases by those who know. The reasons are various, complex, and mostly uninteresting, so I'm not going to wade into explaining. I'm just asking you as a favor to your readers, yourself, and me not to use them.

NOT	BUT
graduated school/college	graduated from school/college
I like/hate/prefer when I like such and such	I like it when or, better, I
appreciate that you	appreciate your or appreciate it when you
same difference	it's all the same
different than	different from
did that already	has/have done that already
unlike in Detroit	unlike the Detroit meeting
unlike when you use a pen	unlike using a pen
as far as [whatever]	as far as [whatever] is concerned, or as for [whatever]

◙ THE BOTTOM LINE ◙

- ▦ **Go easy on capital letters: less is more.**
- ▦ **Put words as close as possible to what they describe.**
- ▦ **Treat abbreviations and acronyms correctly.**
- ▦ **Handle such symbols as # and & cautiously, if at all.**
- ▦ **Edit a few phrases out of your writing permanently.**

APPENDIX A:

Getting Started and Following Through on a Writing Project

Dorothy Parker supposedly once remarked, "Everyone wants to have written, but nobody wants to write." She knew what she was talking about: like another well-known author, Colette, Ms. Parker, a competent author whose way with words is legendary, had to be locked in her room, or so the story goes, before she would actually settle down to the act of writing.

These writers are not alone. Many of us lesser literary lights are plagued by the fear of putting the words down on paper. Why? I'm reminded of a quotation from T. S. Eliot:

> Between the idea
> And the reality
> Between the motion
> And the act
> Falls the Shadow.

I've never known exactly what Eliot was talking about, but for me these words perfectly express the anxiety I feel before I write. I am scared I won't be able to share my idea or argument in a form that will communicate. As grade school children sometimes tell their teachers, "I know the answer—I just can't find the words to say it." Teachers from time immemorial have insisted that if you know what you want to say you can so say it. But I think the children have a point. Sometimes it can be so difficult it's almost threatening to try to find the right words. So difficult, in fact, that we back off from the very act of putting pen to paper or fingertips to keyboard. In fact so threatening that I quit writing this chapter right after the Eliot quotation and spent an hour wandering around the office to no profitable purpose.

Assuming then, that this is a common, not an abnormal, phenomenon, let's examine some strategies to make getting going on a piece of writing easier.

Limit your subject. Don't bite off more than you can chew. This means in every case restricting your own borders to some extent. More important, it means making sure what aspect of the subject the person who asked you to write about it had in mind. Be very sure you know what he or she wants you to focus on. Don't let anyone get away with handing you an unmanageable subject. Both of you need to limit and clarify what's expected. Don't say, "Okay," for example, and dash off to do the job if someone asks you to write a report on temporary employees. The subject could fill the Astrodome. Are we talking about temps in your city? in the state? the United States?

Well, let's assume the person meant the temporary employees in your company. What about them? Their numbers? Their value to the company as compared to the permanent workforce? Their productivity? And so on. Be very sure you and your manager agree on exactly what it is you're meant to be tackling. Otherwise you may do a tremendous amount of work, only to hear the dreaded words, "This isn't what I had in mind."

■ **Be able to state your objective clearly. Be clear about your spin before you write.** Once you're clear on your topic, you can restrict it to the most important areas, rather than wandering down paths that lead nowhere. What is your attitude toward your topic? Know beforehand whether you are going to recommend, blast, try to persuade. This will help define your route through your piece of writing and accordingly lower your fear of what lies ahead in getting it down on paper.

■ **Talk to yourself.** Get a dialogue going, if it doesn't make you feel silly and/or schizophrenic. Who knows? They might give you a private office with a real door! Seriously, many experts advise getting this kind of conversation going as a prelude to writing. Ask yourself such questions as "Why am I writing this? What will convince my reader(s) that my argument is valid? What are the major points I must include? What's the logical order to put them in?" and so on. Oddly enough, this is not only useful, but it functions as a good stress-buster if you have a major load of anxiety about writing the piece.

■ **Collect all the facts you need *before* you begin.** Anxiety may begin or be heightened by the fact that deep inside, you *know* there's an important piece of information you need to complete your letter or report. Do not, I repeat, do not try to write around it or omit it. Sooner or later it's liable to trip you up. If there's a call you need to make, go ahead. Bite the bullet, even if you have to call Mr. Big a third time, talk your way past his assistant, and irritate them both. Leave the office, get in the car, drive back to the library. It's worth it to know you have the facts and are in control of the piece, rather than the other way around.

■ **Get what you want to say down on paper in any form whatsoever.** Think of the information you're loaded down with as a heavy weight. Get rid of it in any way you can. Just throw all the facts on screen or paper before you forget them. Get them down in print. Then you can stop worrying about them. It doesn't matter if they make sense to anyone else: you know what the words mean.

■ **Consider an outline, however brief.** It sounds like grade school, I know, and nobody really wants to write an outline. I hate it, too. But I do it. Go ahead and jot one down. Don't worry about I, II, III, and A, 1, a, i. Just get the scheme in print. It shows you one way to go. If you decide you don't want to go that way, the outline isn't in charge of you, you're in charge of it. Change the outline.

One terrific thing an outline does for you is to help ensure an even depth of focus. Put it up on your Lucite stand or whatever and take a look from time to time as you write. If you've written down three points under the heading "Possible ways to increase sales in rural areas," you're less likely to spend your few precious hours going into minute detail on the first point at the expense of the other two.

■ **Use a template.** Since we know reinventing the wheel isn't smart, and we're all tight on time, why not use a format that has worked in the past for you or someone else in your organization? You can take the bones, or structure, of a successful piece of writing, and infuse that form with your own data. It's not plagiarism, because you're not using the words, or even the ideas, of the other writer. Here are two letters, the template and the "copy":

I. Thank you for allowing me to talk with you about my qualifications for the position of retail operations analyst.

   The opportunity to meet you and Ms. Kahn and to see how your company functions on a daily basis convinces me I'd be able to put my experience to good use at Savignac and Sons.

   I enclose the transcript you requested as well as the names of two references. I look forward to hearing from you.

II. Thank you for participating in the recent focus group sponsored by Fenwick Mutual Life Insurance Company, which investigated why people select various insurance products.

   The answers to the questionnaire you completed, as well as your thoughtful observations during the discussion, will help us serve all our customers better.

As a further way of expressing our thanks for
your participation, I enclose two tickets to the
opening of "Celebrities on Ice" at the City
Center in March. We hope to see you there.

As you can see, the two letters have little in common—except their organization. The writer of II simply
kept the organizational scheme of I and filled in the
blanks. I won't take the space to show you here, but this
can work equally well with a long report. Just be sure
your original template is sound.

■ **Consider the advantages of index or file cards.** It
may sound strange, and it may bring back bad memories
of school reports or worse. I merely said "consider." And
there are a couple of advantages. For one thing, index
cards allow you to manipulate your information physi-
cally in space. You have small bits of discrete data that
can be moved around as necessary, and for those who are
oriented toward the visual and the tactile, this can be
extremely helpful. If you decide to remove some facts,
out they come, but they can sit on a corner of your desk,
readily reinsertable should you change your mind. Also,
as with the outline, if you plan to write about four equally
important projects and see that your stack of cards about
Project B is only half as high as that of Project D, you can
see where your attention should be directed. All this is
possible on a screen, at least in a sense, but it's not really
the same.

If your piece of writing happens to be a speech, your
index cards can move into the final phase with you—right
into the conference room, boardroom, or auditorium.
Cards work well in speeches because they quickly cue

you, and you rarely lose your place, as can happen with a piece of paper.

If you use index cards, especially for a speech, here's one thing to remember: *Be sure to number them* once you get them into their final sequence. I once debated an opponent who dropped her entire stack of cards. As people rushed to help her pick them up, the cards got hopelessly confused; so of course did she, and she lost the debate as a result. (Although I endured some cheap humor afterward, my supporters did not in fact pick up her cards and shuffle them.

■ **Don't resort to delaying tactics.** Let's go about this procedure like adults. Looking up colorful quotations for your opening line is nothing but procrastination in thin disguise. So is checking the Thesaurus on your Tool Bar for synonyms. We've all done it: it's human nature. The problem with it is that it can literally waste hours that you should be spending writing. Yes, you do owe it to yourself to polish your product with these graceful touches—when you arrive at your final draft. Until then, leave blanks, underline poor word choices, write the next thing that comes into your head—do whatever you must to force the enterprise along. **Never try to write perfectly the first time through.** When you're writing your first draft, you're struggling to realize a shape, not burnishing the details.

■ **Take a break. Take a break often.** The coffee break as a right for workers came in with Eleanor Roosevelt. Take advantage of your rights! Medical research shows coffee does in fact make you sharper, up to a point (the point at which you develop the capacity for self-sustained flight). But even more important than the caffeine, a break gives you perspective. If you get away from your work, you'll return to it refreshed and possibly even supplied with new insights.

If you can combine a break with the benefits of oxygen, so much the better. Get outside if possible; go for a brisk walk or a run. The combination of removing yourself from the site of stress and distraction with the endorphins (read "happy hormones") that exercise puts into the bloodstream can produce a mental state of sometimes stunning clarity. I've found the solution to many writing problems, especially those involving organization of a report or arrangement of facts, along the two-mile neighborhood circuit I try to run three times a week.

Don't stop when you're in trouble. I said it's important to take breaks, but I have to highlight one critically important exception. Try never to leave a piece of writing when you've gotten lost. If you paint yourself into a corner where you sense the project has the wrong emphasis, or the writing needs to take a new direction, or it's just gotten so complicated you wonder whether you should throw it out and start over, it's a bad, bad time to take a break. Your reluctance to face the thing again will be tremendous. If this has ever happened to you, you know what I mean. You'll clean out your files before you'll look at that sucker again.

If you're badly stuck, don't walk out. It's far better to hang on until you see the place you want to be, albeit in the distance. Revise your outline. Underline the points you know you've got right. Take a few deep breaths. Then plunge right in again and keep after the copy till you've wrestled it into a shape you can live with. You can take a big break after that. When it's time to get back to work, you'll be glad you didn't quit when you were in trouble.

■ **Visualize success.** Remind yourself how wonderful it feels "to have written." The self-help movement has been high on visualization techniques for a number of years. Borrowing from the trend, I try to visualize the current writing task getting smaller, and smaller, and finally vanishing altogether. And I recollect how utterly terrific I feel when I've completed a big writing assignment. Let yourself dwell on the feeling of relief and accomplishment of having completed a good piece of writing. Contrast it with the grim, gray, guilty way you feel when you have a piece hanging over you. Which feeling weighs more? Which do you prefer?

■ **Let your deadline boost your adrenaline.** Samuel Johnson once said, "When a man knows he is to be hanged in a fortnight, it concentrates his mind wonderfully." For some people, a figurative deadline has the same effect. But for them, two weeks ahead would be way too much time. They prefer to wait until the last minute, then ride the surge of adrenaline from start to finish. These are the people who chronically pulled all-nighters in college. If it works for you, go ahead. For someone my age, it's hard on the system. Besides, you never know: you might get flu or be called out of town. It takes faith to engage in serious procrastination. But you have to do what works for you.

Numbers:
The Basic Rules

It's almost impossible to play the numbers perfectly, because there are dozens of rules and an equally large number of exceptions. You've also got to take the nature of your organization into consideration: if it's a bank or an accounting firm, you may have very different requirements and constraints around the issue from, say, an outplacement bureau or a day care center. Let's try to inject some common sense into this area with a few generally accepted rules for use of numbers in business writing.

Write the numbers one through nine as words; for numbers 10 and up, use numerals. You probably know this rule, and it works pretty well much of the time. If your organization prefers to write out one through twenty, or one through one hundred, that's fine, too. Maintain consistency within your organization if possible, and try to do the same within a piece of writing: that's the most important thing. Now here come all the exceptions to the rule.

■ **Express dates (month and year), street numbers, percentages, decimals, and numbered parts of a document (page, section, etc.) as numerals.** Even if they're below 10, these numbers are traditionally written as numbers, not words. Bet you knew this. Nobody writes "The real estate market had cooled off markedly by *one thousand nine hundred and eighty.*"

> In 1978, in the 1970s, in the '70s
> 111 5th Street
> 3.14195265
> 8 percent
> page 22, section 4

■ **In a series that mixes numbers above and below 10, choose one form.** If you want to advertise round-the-clock customer service, "24 hours a day, seven days a week," while it conforms to our Number One Rule, actually looks capricious and inconsistent. In such a case, either of these is appropriate:

> 24 hours a day, 7 days a week
> twenty-four hours a day, seven days a week

Let your graphic designer be your guide.

■ **However, if you have numbers directly next to one another, you may want to express one as a numeral, the other as a word, to avoid confusion.** For example:

> No: I don't have enough small bills: I need at
> least *100 20s and 50 50s.*
> Yes: I don't have enough small bills: I need at
> least *100 twenties and 50 fifties.*

No: We will need *42¾" lengths* of milled steel to complete this job.

Yes: We will need *forty-two ¾" lengths* of milled steel. . . .

or

We will need *42 three-quarter-inch* lengths of milled steel. . . .

■ **Don't begin a sentence with a number, unless it's a year date.** It looks funny to begin a sentence with a number, like starting with a lowercase letter instead of a capital. Spell out the number or rewrite the sentence:

Ninety thousand shares of XYZ flooded the market.

XYZ flooded the market by selling off *90,000 shares.*

■ **Use figures for all amounts of money.** I strongly recommend this because in business writing, you need to be unambiguous and exact with dollars—or pesos, or pounds. Numerals are clear and unequivocal, and they make a stronger and more durable visual impression than words. While it may make sense to write "fifty cents" in a novel, a bank customer can far more easily comprehend and remember "a $.50 service charge fee" than "a fifty-cent service charge fee." And look at the difference in clarity (and length) between these two sentences:

Sebastian requested an advance of *five hundred and forty-five thousand, seven hundred and fifty dollars.*

Sebastian requested an advance of *$545,750.*

To write out such a number is obviously dumb and unreasonable.

In general, whole numbers of dollars should be expressed without the decimal point and two zeros:

> We will charge *$25* to reconnect your service.

> Three days of defensive driving school will cost *$750* per participant.

However, if you are dealing with a series of mixed dollar amounts (dollars and cents), it's customary to express them all in the same form:

> The company sells the RQ 100 model for *$49.95*; the RQ 150 sells for *$75.00*.

Other exceptions to this convention are dollar and loan amounts in loan and mortgage agreements, wills, and other legal documents, in which exact amounts are critical:

> Title will be transferred concurrent with payment of the sum of *$7,400.00* to Mr. Hugh Dixon.

> You will make 104 payments of *$123.00* each.

■ **Use a comma between groups of three numbers except in year dates.** I'm sure you do this automatically:

> Her estate is estimated to exceed *$14,000,000*.

> I asked her to invoice us in advance for *2,000* copies of the report.

Occasionally people are tempted to omit the comma in a number in the thousands. Resist the temptation and reserve the no-comma convention for year dates:

No: The company now employs over *1000* analysts.

Yes: The company now employs over *1,000* analysts.

But: Our computers already deal ably with the year *2000*.

In *1945,* butter was difficult to obtain all over the country.

■ **In most cases, write days of the month as numerals.** *February 23, 1979*. That's just the way it's done. Although dates are pronounced as ordinals (the descriptive, *-st, -nd, -rd* forms of numbers), don't write *September 23rd* or *June 1st*:

On *September 23,* 1948, the organization was incorporated.

May we expect a decision by *June 1?*

However, you may use the ordinal forms if the order of the date is inverted, or if no month is specified:

We are closed on *the fourth of July.*

I will expect your answer before *the 21st.*

■ **Write out numbers above nine.** If you do need to write them out as words, the numbers twenty-one through twenty-nine, thirty-one through thirty-nine, and so on, up through ninety-one through ninety-nine, are hyphenated. The rest—one hundred, one thousand, one hundred thousand—are written without hyphens. The ordinals—twenty-first through twenty-ninth, and so on—work the same way:

Thirty-eight thousand runners participated in the *one hundredth* running of the Boston Marathon.

■ **Follow this rule for fractions.** Leave them open when they are nouns, hyphenate them as adjectives:

Noun: Fidelity placed *one half* of the Salem municipal bonds traded in May.

Adjective: We need a *two-thirds majority* to carry the resolution.

■ **Express the time of day as a number.** Again, this recommendation is specific to business writing: you're less likely to be misunderstood and more likely to be remembered:

I've scheduled the meeting for *7:45 P.M.*

Kate will be here before *9:00* and after *11:30.*

■ **Don't create hybrid forms in a range of inclusive numbers.** When you want to express the idea of duration or inclusion within a certain range of numbers, you have a couple of options. If, for example, your intern Josh was in a five-day management seminar, you have at least three acceptable ways of expressing the fact:

Josh attended the seminar January *1–5.*

Josh attended the seminar *from* January 1 *to* January 5.

Josh attended the seminar *between* January 1 *and* January 5.

The first form, with the en dash, is informal, the others stricter style. The pitfall inherent in having choices is that people often unwisely try to combine two styles. You should not write, for example:

Josh attended the seminar *from January 1–5.*

or

Josh attended the seminar *between January 1–5.*

Either go with the en dash and no words or use both words: *from . . . to, between . . . and.*

APPENDIX C:

A Word About Your Computer

Y ou probably write on a PC or laptop, using one of the standard word processors. Your word processing software includes tools you can use to help improve your prose, but you must take them with what my great-aunt Jane, whose life was a monument to malapropisms, used to call "a dose of salts." You must under no circumstances rely on them to eliminate writing errors. I'm not denying they can help, but the computer cannot think the way a person does. Sorry: a computer cannot think at all. (Not yet, anyhow.) Here are some recommendations for making use of the strengths while avoiding the weaknesses of these tools.

■ **Grammar checkers.** Grammar checkers flag such common errors as disagreement, sentence fragments, and overreliance on passive construction. Given the complexity of our language, it's amazing that they work at all, and I find they don't work very well. The Grammar tool on my menu bar can't distinguish between the two uses of *many* in the following sentences, for example:

Many thanks for agreeing to represent Foss Brothers.

Some of these parts are built to spec, but *many* are not.

Grammar suggested that the former sentence should read "Many *thank*. . . ." I don't think so. I really don't blame the creators of Grammar and its like—it's remarkable that these programs are as good as they are—but I don't trust their creations either.

Naturally, because programming is an all-or-nothing business, Grammar is hypervigilant. This can be profoundly annoying. The moment it runs across any form of the verb *to be,* it suspects a passive construction. I've suggested you do the same, but you're better off running your own check than having Grammar wag a finger every time you say, "I am pleased," or "I'm worried."

Sometimes a call is just plain wrong, often almost inexplicably. For example, Grammar flagged this sentence as containing subject-verb disagreement:

I hope you and Adelaide have a productive meeting.

It suggests the sentence should read "*has* a productive meeting." What can I say? It also stumbled on the phrase "those papers that," suggesting that I consider "that papers that" or "those paper that." Possibly it took *paper* as a verb.

And if you use the phrases, "in fact," "in general," or "as you are aware," Grammar notes that you should avoid clichés. Well, maybe, if you're using them seven times in a one-page letter—but they're fairly harmless used once or twice.

Bottom line: grammar checkers can be helpful, but they have clear limitations. Stay tuned. Somewhere out there, perhaps in a humble garage, Weird Stanley, the Programmer Who Has No Life, is developing a version that can deal with all these shortcomings, and more.

■ **Spell checkers.** You've probably experienced the limitations of these tools already. Spell checkers can set you right if you misspell a word: they're all over *acommodate, accomodate,* and *acommoddate.* They've also been creatively programmed to figure out just what it was you were trying to spell. But they don't have a hope if you misuse a word. Homonyms—words that sound alike but have different meanings and spellings—are all the same to them. *Their, there,* and *they're* are equally acceptable to my spell checker. And it's perfectly content with such atrocities as

> Legal council argues that this elicit behavior mitigates against hiring are allusive applicant.

It's also unable to recognize the nonsense created by extraneous words, often the result of hasty editing:

> I must get a flight to for Detroit immediately.

(Interestingly, my grammar checker finds nothing wrong with that sentence, either, and gives it excellent scores for readability. Weird Stanley better get cracking.)

Spell checkers can be meddlesome, too. Copyeditors for a recent bestseller cooperatively changed the spelling of Scituate, a town in Massachusetts, to "Situate," a word the spell checker recognized. The locals are offended and the author is embarrassed.

On the plus side, my spell checker lifts my spirits by offering some wonderful suggestions for proper names it doesn't recognize, offering "carboy" for "Kirby" and archly recommending "hoyden" for "Hayden." This is almost more fun than solitaire.

■ **Grade or reading level indicators.** Your software may include various types of readability gauges, alone or as part of your grammar checker. The five or six I've seen scan your piece for variables such as word length and passive constructions. By collating the data, they arrive at a numerical score that supposedly reflects the readability of your prose.

The late Robert Gunning's Fog Index is as reliable as any, but it's helpful only if you can interpret the results. My word processor simply gives me a score with no explanation in the manual or the program. I offered it two paragraphs, one very simple, one very difficult, and received respective scores of 0 and 30. This paragraph scored a 13.2; random paragraphs in this book tend to land between 8 and 12. If your Gunning Fog Index came without an explanation, this gives you an idea of where to aim.

Readability indexes aren't entirely dependable. I understand one of them gave Lincoln's Gettysburg Address and a passage from Mark Twain's *Huckleberry Finn* very bad reviews. That's enough to erode my confidence. The message: use readability indexes if you like, but don't let them push you around.

■ **Replace and Find Commands.** Most word processing software helps you quickly find and replace a word you've used, presumably because you're having second thoughts about it. If you use your Replace command, remember that it will replace a word but may leave extraneous material behind, such as a final *s* if you've made a possessive plural, that is no longer appropriate. Another problem is that most Replace commands will not replace any word that has a punctuation mark after it, no matter how you instruct them, because they don't recognize the word with the punctuation as the same word you're asking to replace. So if you're replacing, you're going to have to run a spell check, and you probably should read through the text yourself as well. In other words, you might as well have used the Find command and replaced the words yourself one by one. As for Find, if I accidentally insert a space in my Find What box (it's hard to see when you've done it), my program is unable to find the word or phrase unless the word in text happens to have an extra space in the same place.

My point is that all these tools, while they can be useful, can also waste your time. Worse, if you are foolish enough to depend upon them, they can give you a false sense of security. As of this writing, they're no substitute for your own thoughtful editing.

A Special Situation: Responding to Customer Complaint Letters

Since no organization is perfect, inevitably you'll get them—the dreaded letters of complaint. Here are some tips to ensure that your response satisfies the writer of a complaint to you or to your organization.

■ **Follow a policy of responding immediately to a complaint.** Remember, your writer is already dissatisfied and has gone to the trouble of writing and sending a letter. The only payback in delaying your answer is increased resentment. If you're charged with responding to a complaint, don't wait. If you can't get into the issue immediately, or if the problem is particularly complex, write or phone the customer to say you've received the letter and will be responding as soon as possible.

In some large organizations, a letter of complaint prompts a form letter signed by a member of senior management, often the president. This letter goes out immediately to the customer, expressing thanks for his or her communication and voicing assurances that the matter is being looked into. It doesn't need to be long (see First Response to Customer Complaint, page 204). The form letter is followed up quickly by a letter that specifically addresses the issue(s) the customer has raised.

■ **Read the customer's letter very, very carefully.** You want to be sure you understand just what has upset the person and interpret what the letter says as accurately as possible. Try to keep your own feelings and projections out of your reading so you don't overreact or respond to an issue that hasn't even been raised. Be sure you completely understand the problem or problems: often a letter highlights more than one.

■ **Remind yourself that your customer is your superior.** Business texts make the point that your customer is by definition up the organizational chain from you. Use the information in Chapter 3 to generate a tone that is respectful and polite. Never blame or belittle a customer—even a customer who is wrong. That's just not good politics.

■ **Look at the issue from the customer's viewpoint.** It's no use telling the customer, for example, that slow service reflects recent layoffs designed to save the company money. That's writer centered, and it's just going to anger the customer further. Avoid references to job productivity, performance goals, and other similar concepts that reflect the organization's viewpoint. Concentrate, instead, on the effect on the customer: the customer's feelings, convenience, time wasted, money lost, etc. In this way, you can project empathy that goes a long way toward defusing anger.

▪ **Try to understand where the letter is coming from.**
Here's where a little armchair psychology can help you.
Learn all you can about the writer through his or her letter. By reading thoughtfully, you can get inside the
writer's head and perhaps figure out whether the person
is

> rational
> lonely
> hostile and taking it out on you
> well educated
> crazy (it happens: be careful)
> young and inexperienced
> old and puzzled

and tailor your response accordingly.

▪ **Be aware that you are documenting, on behalf of
yourself and your organization.** Don't say anything you
may later regret. Remember that your reply represents a
commitment. If you agree to a condition the customer
requests, or offer a rebate or reimbursement by way of
apology, be sure your organization will stand behind you.

▪ **Explain why you are the person responding if the
customer's letter was written to someone else.** Most
letters are written to senior management; most are
answered by someone less senior. Show why you are the
appropriate person to answer the letter:

> Because I'm in charge of environmental compli-
> ance at BCX, Mr. Henshaw has forwarded your
> letter to me, and I am pleased to have the chance
> to respond to your concerns.

■ **Show you understand by walking the customer through the episode(s).** Let's say, for example, you handle complaints for a brokerage firm. A customer placed a stock trade that somehow was not completed, called to inquire about it, and was first put on hold, then disconnected. Reflect each part of the experience back to the customer in your letter:

> I understand that you placed a trade for 2,000 shares of NetWorth on December 18 at 10:00 A.M. Apparently, our organization failed to complete your trade. The next day, NetWorth rose 46 points, or 50 percent. When you called on December 21 to sell, you discovered the trade had never been placed. And when you asked to speak to a supervisor, your call was delayed and ultimately disconnected. . . .

People sometimes object when I tell them to do this. They are afraid the customer will only get increasingly riled up if they start going over the ground again. I disagree, because I've spoken with a number of customers about the technique, and virtually all endorse it. It confirms that someone has read their letter with care. It also serves as an acknowledgment of what took place, which will lead to an explanation, at least, if not an apology. For the example above, let's hope someone can produce one eloquent enough to forestall a lawsuit.

■ **Explain what happened and why.** Your reader will appreciate a well-reasoned explanation of the episode. You should take particular care to pitch this explanation at a level that's understandable to someone outside the organization. No jargon, no telescoping of procedures: remember the Dangerous Level of Knowledge. Your reader doesn't know this material the way you do.

■ **Be open rather than defensive. If your organization blew it, apologize.** This advice, which I've given before, is worth repeating. Nobody's perfect, and you and your company are no exception. It's painful to have to admit to a mistake. But from the customer's standpoint, it's much easier to forgive someone who is openly and sincerely apologizing than someone making excuses. Trying to cover up or justify an error only makes the problem worse and the customer angrier.

Be sure, if your customer has two gripes, that you apologize for both.

■ **Try to give the customer something if you've caused a problem.** Of course you'll substitute a product that works for one that doesn't. If you overcharged, you'll refund or rebate the charge. And if there may still be any possible confusion or questions in the customer's mind, you'll give your phone number or that of someone down the chain so the customer will have an immediate contact within the organization.

But consider, in addition, if you've caused real inconvenience, the possibility of giving the customer something—in short, a present. Some organizations have small gifts ready to give out in such situations, from digital clocks to mouse pads to T-shirts, often printed with the company logo. It's not so much the value of the item as the symbolic gesture of good will. Other companies will reduce a price or payment if the customer has been seriously inconvenienced. A dreadful clerk in a department store once gave me a runaround that included rude behavior and inaccurate information about the item I wanted to buy. I finally took the item to the manager, who apologized wholeheartedly, then rang up the item for me at half price. He hoped, he said, it would in some measure make up for the inconvenience I had suffered. And it did. About 100 percent. As the song says, money changes everything: consider it when you want to assuage a complaint.

■ **Take steps within your organization so this won't happen again.** Well, so it's at least less likely to happen again. Your job's not over when you've resolved the problem to a customer's satisfaction. A customer's complaint may also signal a weakness within some area of your business or company that if addressed could improve your performance overall. If appropriate, you may want to write a memo to whoever's responsible for the management of that area. A customer writing about a poorly performing appliance, for example, could help alert a company to problems on its production line. If a customer complains about incompetent service, the complaint could point to larger issues of hiring practices, adequate staffing, or proper training.

First Response to Customer Complaint
(form letter with blanks filled in)

Xavier Marine Products
412 Lynn Avenue
Seattle, Washington 98199

March 17, 19__

Mr. Jacob Goodwin
3906 Indian Lane
Washington, DC 20008

Dear Mr. Goodwin:

Thank you for your letter of March 16, in which you express concerns about our radio direction finder, which apparently directed you into a cranberry bog instead of the Cape Cod Canal. Because at Xavier Marine Products we are eager to deliver the best possible service to our customers, we appreciate it when a customer who experiences problems calls them to our attention. We are looking into the matter, and you can expect to hear from us within a week.

Sincerely,

Bert Samuelson, President
Xavier Marine Products

Response to Customer Complaint

Third Citizens Bank
800 Washington Boulevard
Minneapolis, Minnesota

August 22, 19___

Ms. Lucy Robbins
252 Overlook Drive
Hyde Park, NY 12538

Dear Ms. Robbins:

Thank you for your recent letter to Third Citizens. I am sorry that you have been perplexed regarding the figure owed and the late payment charge on your installment loan account. And I apologize sincerely, on behalf of Citizens, for the difficult time you have had trying to get a satisfactory explanation to the problem. The enclosed account payment history should help answer some of your questions.

You asked why you owe $102.73 and why you are being charged for a late payment. On this type of loan, additional funds received are not applied to the balance but are credited toward the next scheduled payment. On June 4, 19___, we received your check (number 1435) for $521.73. The amount due was $309.73, leaving extra funds of $212.00. This extra amount was "rolled over" toward your next payment date, leaving $97.73 due to complete a full payment. A late charge of $5.00 was added to that $97.73, bringing the total amount due to complete that partial payment to $102.73. This is why you are receiving letters requesting that amount.

I apologize for the inconvenience you experienced when you telephoned on July 15, were put on hold, waited for 10 minutes, and ultimately received no satisfactory answer to your questions. I have spoken with the customer service representatives on duty that day, reminding them of their obligation to be helpful and courteous to all customers. We also reviewed the procedure for installment loan overpayments and late charges to help ensure others are served properly in the future. Thank you for bringing the matter to our attention. Although we try to give our customers excellent service, despite our best efforts, we occasionally fall short of our goal, as we evidently did on this occasion. Again, my apologies.

If you have further questions about your loan payments, please call me at any time. My telephone number is 602-374-3206.

Sincerely,

Katherine Smallzell
Vice President

APPENDIX E:

Memo and Letter Tips and Formats

If your organization has formats you're asked to follow, so much the better. If not, and particularly if people are doing their own thing and stuff is being sent around to other departments or into the outside world at the whim of individual writers, you may want to standardize letter and memo formats. This saves time, once everyone knows exactly what's expected. No one needs to call around or dig out the Katie Gibbs manual that was right there on the receptionist's desk before she went on vacation. You'll also present an image of yourselves as well organized and in control.

The following tips will remind you of what readers deserve in a memo or letter. The sample formats reflect my years of thinking about what looks nice, observing what various organizations do, and selectively checking out secretarial handbooks and business style manuals. Most of these give any number of possible formats: evidently there really isn't one "correct" form. Just choose one and stick with it. I happen to like these two.

TIPS FOR MEMO WRITING

- Make certain your subject heading is explanatory—a headline, not a title.
- Keep to a single subject whenever possible.
- Try to limit your memo to a single page.
- Put points in logical sequence. Be accurate and specific with details.
- Since a memo is typically an internal communication, your language should pass the read-aloud test without embarrassing you: make it simple and conversational.
- At closing, prompt any necessary action from your reader(s).
- Note any attachment; note copies sent to anyone else.
- Double-check for mechanical errors.

SAMPLE MEMO FORMAT

(Letterhead, if desired)
Third Citizens Five Cents Bank, N.A.

(Skip three spaces)
TO: Jane Upshaw
(Skip one space)
FROM: David Thorne
(Skip one space)
SUBJECT: Alexander Hamilton School of Banking
"Scholarships"
(Skip one space)
DATE: March 2, 19__

(Skip three spaces. Begin body copy, block style, no indent)
I recommend that we earmark approximately $50,000 of next year's Education Required Budget to begin a systematic process of sponsoring two key Citizens staff members as students in the Alexander Hamilton School of Banking (AHSB). As this is a three-year program, we'll need to have a comparable amount allocated in subsequent years (see proposed budget outline, attached).
(Skip one space)
AHSB offers a curriculum designed to provide depth in management ranks. It focuses on bankers with expertise in their own specialized areas and broadens their experience to include other areas of banking. In addition, the AHSB program requires a thesis, and many participants have apparently used this opportunity to develop frameworks for new programs to be implemented in their own banks.

(Skip one space)

If you like the idea, I recommend that we ask Mary Dale, John McAllister, and Arthur Beal to consider areas of their departments where management depth is a concern. Then, either through an application process or personal recommendations, we can create a pool of candidates. Final selections can be made by a panel of Human Resources senior management, in-house AHSB graduates, and line management.

(Skip one space)

Please let me know your thoughts. The deadline for early admissions is November 15.

(Skip five spaces)

Attachment

(Skip one space)

cc: Eleanor Wu
　　Dan Paulsen

TIPS ON WRITING LETTERS

- Use a colon after your salutation, even after a first name.
- Don't waste your opening line: open graciously.
- Share good news immediately.
- Hold bad news until you've built your case.
- Use "I" and "you" freely, focusing on "you."
- Don't use formal language or outdated business idioms.
- Close politely: suggest next step or contact, then, if appropriate, voice appreciation of reader and indicate your pleasure to serve, help, share.
- Make note of enclosures and copies.
- Reread your letter for errors, sound effects.
- Reread again to be sure it *clearly* answers the question, "Why this letter?"

SAMPLE LETTER FORMAT

(Letterhead) Custom Structured Systems
3 Pinecliffe Drive, Winchester, Illinois 60914

(skip 6 spaces)

June 18, 19___

(skip three spaces)

Mr. Thomas Wright, President
Wright Investments, Inc.
1444 5th Street
Chicago, IL 60912
(skip one space)
Dear Mr. Wright:
(skip one space. Begin body copy, block style, no indents)
I'm pleased to respond to your invitation to undertake work for Wright Investments. Custom Structured Systems (CSS) proposes to perform a data processing study and prepare a report that will recommend the most effective new computer system for Wright. I've enclosed a Statement of Work that describes the specific tasks CSS will perform as part of this effort.
(skip one space)
Our study will focus on understanding and defining your present and future data processing needs and choosing the computers and applications that best meet those needs.
(skip one space)
We'll analyze Wright's business operations and current systems and evaluate appropriate computers and appli-

cation programs. Based on our findings, we'll then recommend the most effective system for Wright and present a detailed plan for an orderly conversion of your existing computer applications.

(skip one space)

Please let me know whether this proposal meets with your approval. CSS is eager to begin the study, and we look forward to working with Wright.

(skip two spaces)

Sincerely,

(skip four spaces)

Martha N. Briedis
Senior Vice President

(skip two spaces)

MNB/db (writer's and secretary's initials, if appropriate)
(skip one space)
Enclosure
(skip one space)
cc (or *xc* for Xerox copy, or simply *c*):   John Lee

APPENDIX F:

Other Books on Writing

Books Targeted Specifically to Business Writing

Brusaw, Charles, *et al. The Business Writer's Handbook*, 4th ed., revised. New York: St. Martin's Press, 1993. This one's been around for a long time and reflects good common sense and straightforward advice. It's very thorough, and also kind of a workout, which fits some people's needs: its 800 pages include a lot of exercises and examples.

Dumaine, Deborah. *Write to the Top: Writing for Corporate Success*. New York: Random House, Inc., 1989. Short, upbeat, and easy to read, this book offers practical advice on writing in the business place and amusing examples of bad letters and memos. Among its exercises is a useful set that helps you assess your own writing strengths and weaknesses.

Fielden, John, and Ronald Dulek. *Bottom-Line Business Writing*. Englewood Cliffs, N.J.: Prentice-Hall, Inc., 1984. A small, well-written book with some interesting ideas and theories about what to write to whom and when. Emphatically oriented toward the structure rather than the mechanics of writing, it examines in depth the form and language appropriate for memos, letters, and reports, depending on the relative positions of writer and reader in the organizational hierarchy.

Geffner, Andrea B. *Business English: A Complete Guide,* 3rd ed. Hauppauge, N.Y.: Barron's Educational Series, 1998. This is a large, comprehensive paperback, written for a general business audience. It spends a lot of time on the elementary: parts of speech, principles of grammar and punctuation, how to spell the plurals of words ending in -*s,* and the like. Lots of exercises, with answers, reinforce its guidelines. It also includes dozens of model letters, memos, and reports on very specific topics: Letter Declining a Job Offer, Credit-Refusing Letter, even a business Letter of Condolence.

Tarshis, Barry. *Grammar for Smart People.* New York: Pocketbooks, 1993. My favorite newsletter editor swears by this one for grammar and punctuation. Barry Tarshis writes appealingly and straightforwardly. An easy read, well targeted for a business audience.

BOOKS ON WRITING IN GENERAL

The Associated Press Stylebook and Libel Manual, 6th ed. Reading, Mass.: Addison-Wesley, 1996. I don't recommend this as an all-round bible. It works well if you're a journalist, but the style is less strict than most manuals suggest for business use. Relaxed style may work well for a newspaper or magazine, but it could get you into trouble on the job. Compare your morning paper and you'll see what I mean: mine makes inconsistent use of the serial comma, drops the *s* after possessive nouns ending in *s,* and in general commits errors you don't want to make.

On the other hand, the AP Stylebook section gives useful information on treatment of words and names, pointing out that Hovercraft is a trademark, that the U.S. Census divides the Northeast region into the New England and the Middle Atlantic states, and that *prior to* is a stilted version of *before.* In addition to the Libel Manual, it includes, among other things, a short but helpful glossary of business terms.

Bernstein, Theodore M. *The Careful Writer.* New York: Simon & Schuster, 1977. This book is a classic, wonderful and informative, a pleasure to read for its own sake. The late Theodore Bernstein was a star in the pantheon of writing experts, and his writing is funny as well as authoritative. His commonsense approach seems as reasonable as when the book first appeared in 1965. *The Careful Writer* is encyclopedic in form—that is, it goes from A to Z—and I virtually always find what I'm looking for in it. Did you know the word *deficient* takes the preposition *in?* or that *postpone* and *delay* don't mean the same thing? Read this and learn more from a widely respected author and editor.

Buckley, William F., Jr. *The Right Word.* Selected, assembled, and edited by Samuel S. Vaughan. New York: Random House, 1996. The feisty editor of *National Review* as revealed in correspondence, interviews, fiction, and essays, with his take on words from every angle: punctuation, usage, gender-blind writing, dictionaries, fax, and e-mail—you name it. Approximately one hundred pages comprise a "Buckley Lexicon": anyone who'd like to build a more graceful vocabulary should take note.

Buckley yields to no one in the elegance with which he expresses himself.

Chicago Manual of Style, 14th ed. Chicago: University of Chicago Press, 1993. Probably the ultimate in comprehensive and authoritative. This book undertakes to guide the reader in writing a book or thesis: from its inception, through the complexities of tables of contents, footnotes, and indexes, to publication. It offers the last word on capitalization, forms of address for members of governments around the world, punctuation (20 different sections on use of the comma and 13 pages on the hyphen). It's very well indexed and thorough; for business purposes, it offers much more than you need to know, but it's an invaluable resource.

Fowler, H. W. *A Dictionary of Modern English Usage.* 3rd ed., edited by R.W. Burchfield. Oxford: Oxford University Press, 1996. Another classic, this one recently revised and updated. The first edition, published in 1926 and more recently revised by Ernest Gowers, reflected the author's unique take on usage and method of indexing, which included such entries as "Airs and graces" and "Pleonastic humor." The mode of organization has always made it hard to find what you're looking for in Fowler. The new edition has simplified getting around the book somewhat, but it has been faulted for laxity in style: its acceptance of "impact" as a verb, for example, and "hopefully" meaning "it is to be hoped." Many of the original, quirky Fowlerisms remain, however, and the book is fun for browsing.

Hodges, John C., *et al. Harbrace College Handbook,* 11th ed. San Diego: Harcourt Brace Jovanovich, Inc., 1990. A serviceable text focusing on grammar, style, and usage. Many other large publishing houses issue similar ones, also well done. There's more basic information in them than you may need, but it's all there if you do.

Johnson, Edward. *The Handbook of Good English.* New York: Washington Square Press, 1991. I stumbled accidentally on this thorough and carefully written handbook on grammar, style, and usage and now use it often. Edward Johnson's system of sections confuses me a little, but that may be my fault for always being in a hurry. His comprehensive glossary, which also functions as an index, helps. The book contains a lot of excellent information covered in painstaking detail.

Safire, William. *On Language.* New York: Times Books, 1980. The *New York Times* columnist is arguably the most widely read writer on language in the world. Even non-writerly types love his Sunday column. If you want to read about jargon, slang, dialect, or new words, you'll find any of Safire's books witty and enjoyable. In *On Language*, he blends material from his columns with letters from readers, to entertaining effect.

Strunk, William, and E. B. White. *The Elements of Style*, 3rd ed. Boston: Allyn & Bacon, 1979. Some things don't change. Strunk and White has been in its third edition for nearly 20 years: why shouldn't it be? It's timeless. It hits the high spots of writing in general in just 92 pages of clear, sensible prose. The book is particularly targeted to college students, for whom it was originally written, but the advice applies to all types of writing.

Turabian, Kate. *A Manual for Writers of Term Papers, Theses, and Dissertations,* 6th ed. Chicago: University of Chicago Press, 1996. A short paperback based on the *Chicago Manual of Style,* this book contains easy-to-understand, decisive information. Spelling and Punctuation, and Capitalization, Underlining, and Other Matters of Style are among its most useful chapters. The punctuation sections are particularly comprehensive and comprehensible. Offered as "the definitive guide on correct style for formal papers," the book is obviously meant for scholars, and one can't follow its guidelines to the letter in all types of business writing (advertising, for example), but it provides an excellent base from which to start.

Words Into Type, 4th ed., edited by Thomas L. Warren. Englewood Cliffs: Prentice-Hall, Inc., 1992. Get this one for the office. My third edition (based on studies by Marjorie Skillen *et al.*) has served me so well I'm going to stick with it. A fairly expensive hardcover book, it bails me out when I run into tough editing problems, be they ever so tiny or downright weird. Where else can you find nearly a page of discussion of nouns with two different plurals, or the proper abbreviations for all the Canadian provinces? My *Words Into Type* includes a large section on grammar; long and helpful lists on such subjects as Trite Expressions, Words and Phrases Often Used Superfluously, and Foreign Words and Phrases; and a 14-page section on The Right Preposition! To add to its charms, the book is indexed in a way that seems both complete and intuitive.

Zinsser, William. *On Writing Well: An Informal Guide to Writing Nonfiction,* 5th ed., revised and updated. New York: Harper/Collins College, 1995. Open any page and you'll be hooked. Everyone seems to love Mr. Zinsser's writing: this book has been on everyone's recommended list for decades. His examples of writing are lively as well as instructive, and he has a chapter on business writing that glows with wisdom.

DICTIONARIES

American Heritage Dictionary of the English Language, 3rd ed. Boston: Houghton Mifflin Company, 1994. This comprehensive dictionary includes the recommendations of the Usage Panel, including the percentages who sponsor or shun a particular element of style or usage. The Usage Panel comprises a collection of writers, editors, and other experts, and its notes, uniformly lively and interesting, represent an admirable blend of tradition and common sense.

Merriam-Webster's Collegiate Dictionary. Springfield, MA: Merriam-Webster, 1996 or latest version. This is the short version of *Webster's Third New International Unabridged Dictionary* and is the choice of the *Chicago Manual of Style* for all questions of spelling and word division. That's good enough for me. It has the additional charm of telling you when a word came into use: *normalcy* has been with us since 1857, believe it or not. It also gives long lists of words with prefixes such as *pre-* and *non-* that it suggests not hyphenating. Make everyone in the department use this dictionary: you'll present a consistent image because you'll all be, literally, on the same page.

Index